DISCARD

MICHAEL SYMON'S
LIVE TO COOK

MICHAEL SYMON'S LIVE TO COOK

RECIPES AND TECHNIQUES TO ROCK YOUR KITCHEN

MICHAEL SYMON WITH MICHAEL RUHLMAN

FOREWORD BY BOBBY FLAY

Clarkson Potter/Publishers
NEW YORK

ACKNOWLEDGEMENTS

No chef gets anywhere without a fleet of people behind him and in this I've been incredibly lucky, truly blessed with great family, an amazing wife, and an excellent staff, people who have stayed with me for so many years in a transitory industry.

I want to thank my mom, Angel, my dad, Dennis, my sister, Nikki, and my grandparents, who made cooking and eating together a pleasure from the beginning. Of course I want to thank Lizzie and Kyle. I was lucky beyond words that Liz happened to be working at the place where I found my first job out of culinary school. I'd like to thank Lizzie's parents as well, Russ and Sherla. Thank you, Doug Petkovic, one of my oldest and dearest friends, who became my business partners. And I can't forget James Sammon, best friend, and more important, my lawyer, who, God bless him, has traded countless legal-work hours for food.

I'm grateful to my staff and chefs, past and present, especially Frank Rogers, Matt Harlan, Derek Clayton, Cory Barrett, Jeff Rose, Jonathon Sawyer, and Jon Seeholzer. They're the ones who truly keep the businesses running. And my great assistant, Rebecca Yodi, keeps me running. They've become family too.

Thank you Scott Feldman and all the folks at 212 Management, and I also want to say thanks to my Food Network family.

Books, like restaurants, take a team of people, and I'm grateful to all the people who helped to make this book happen: Michael and Donna Ruhlman and Heidi Robb here in Cleveland, and in New York, my agent, Elizabeth Kaplan, and my editor, Rica Allannic; creative director, Marysarah Quinn; managing editor, Amy Boorstein; and production manager, Kim Tyner.

To all, thank you.

Cont

ents

Foreword

By Bobby Flay

Michael Symon is cooking . . . that means the aroma of sizzling pork is in the air!

Michael Symon is a good friend of mine, and that makes me a lucky guy. When he asked me to write this Foreword I was flattered, in part due to my respect for his food and his personality, but also because any chef Michael has come into contact with over the years would have been honored to contribute to this, his first cookbook.

Chef Symon and his coauthor, Michael Ruhlman, give you all you need to know to emulate the Symon way of cooking and eating, which is a good thing. Now because I have had the privilege of spending plenty of quality time with him, I am going to try to let you in on who Michael Symon really is—as a chef, as a cook, and as a friend.

Michael Symon loves to ride motorcycles, although he recently admitted to me that his current maturity has him less behind the handlebars and more likely to be gripping a golf club these days. (For those who are interested, he's about a nine handicap on a good day, so beware!) He has also traded in his competitive wrestling gear for an Iron Chef jersey, which makes him rather dangerous in Kitchen Stadium. Instead of putting his competitors in a devastating headlock, he is now more likely to bring them to their knees with a bowl of crispy gnocchi with morels and peas.

Michael knows who he is and where he lives, and his heritage and community come into play in his deeply personal, soul-satisfying dishes. The thing I love most about Michael's food is that it's handcrafted and focused, and each dish has a distinct story to tell.

Michael's pedigree is predominantly Greek and Italian, so his food often tastes like it's been flown in from the Mediterranean. You'll find lots of Greek yogurt, tons of lemon, fish cooked in grape leaves, and handfuls of savory pastas to fill your table.

Since he lives in Cleveland, Ohio (which, by the way, makes him a huge fan of the Cleveland Cavaliers and Cleveland Browns, and he roots as hard as anyone I've seen), his Midwestern sensibilities also come into play when he cooks. Michael encourages not only flavor but also abundance and embraces dishes like pierogies, an Eastern European answer to the dumpling, which he fills with beef cheeks and laces with horseradish. He also shares a full roster of sausages and charcuterie that tie his Midwestern pride to his olive oil bloodline.

Chef Symon isn't just obsessed with pork—it's a part of his lifestyle. He doesn't just teach you how to cook a pork chop or two—although I am looking forward to checking out his rack of pork with grilled peaches and chestnut honey—Michael uses pork as his "ace in the hole," a card he plays often and with tremendous results. He uses pork cheeks in chili, braises greens with bacon, pairs pork belly with polenta and wild mushrooms, and wraps walleye in bacon. He hits a pork double in something he calls a "BBLT," which combines pork belly and bacon. Then there's the puree of pea soup, which he uses as a canvas for three pork provisions: bacon, ham hocks, and spare ribs. I say: Bring it! And for lots of fun, let's not forget the crispy pig ears! Could any other recipe prove just how dedicated he is to embracing every last edible part of his beloved pig? You may have reservations now, but believe me—Michael will make a convert out of you.

Michael is always easy to find in a crew; just listen for his infectious laugh, a signature of his genuine personality. He is high energy and good humored, with a heart of gold and a passion for all things delicious. Michael is the cook you want guiding you in your own kitchen. Just listen to what Symon says! I promise it will be worth it.

Introduction

It's been a fact of my life and of my work, and it's one of the most important things I know: food brings people together.

I grew up in a family that loves food and truly loves to cook. My mom, Angel, born to Greek and Italian parents, always cooked from scratch when I was a kid and, with one exception I'll explain, I don't remember a time when we didn't sit down together to eat and talk about the day. Importantly, all the *men* in my family were great cooks, too. My dad, Dennis, has roots in what is now Ukraine. And so I was raised with this Greek-Italian-Slovakian-melting-pot food mentality.

When I say that I was fortunate to grow up in a family that loved to cook and gathered at the table every night, it's no small statement. In fact, it's the primary influence in my life as a chef; it determined who I am and the food I cook. All those meals I ate growing up, those aromas from the kitchen.

Of course there were professional culinary influences—gleaned from cooking school, from Cleveland chefs under whom I apprenticed, and from chefs beyond who became my colleagues, such as Jonathan Waxman and Bobby Flay—but all of the learning sits on the big rock of what I call heritage food, the food given to me by my mom and dad and their families in North Olmstead, a working-class suburb of Cleveland.

The weekday food growing up was from Mom—lasagna, braised beef, pork neck ragù—big hearty meals served family-style at a dinner table that often featured friends from the block. My dad was a night-shift manager at a Ford auto plant, but he was able to eat with us before heading to work, and when we were getting up, he'd be getting home—hungry for potato pancakes or amazing salami sandwiches.

Weekends throughout my childhood, my dad's dad, Pap, a pipefitter, would take me to Cleveland's extraordinary West Side Market, purpose-built in 1912 and still thriving, to gather sausages and potatoes and slabs of ribs and smoked ham hocks. We'd spend all day cooking pierogies and split pea soup with braised ribs and ham hocks. I make a lot of fancy food as a restaurant chef, but at heart I am that pork-filled soup, a soppressata sandwich with a fried egg on top, Italian braised beef, or the great lamb meatballs that were a staple at family gatherings. I've built my career on family food.

With all this amazing food around, it's ironic that I spent half the winters of my youth preventing myself from eating it. I went to one of the state's powerhouse sports schools, St. Ed's, and I was a fanatically competitive wrestler. I spent the years from age twelve to sixteen trying to make weight—105 pounds (hard to believe given my current, uh, stature). My family knew how I loved to eat and how hard this was for me during the season, so they'd actually plan dinners to coincide with my practice, when I wasn't around. Food brings people together, and I saw the reverse was also true: in depriving myself of food, I deprived myself of family. During the winters, Mom would wipe down every inch of the kitchen after dinner and open all the windows to air out the house so there wouldn't be a trace of her food when I got home and I wouldn't feel so hungry. She understood the power of food.

At sixteen, in a wrestling practice, I broke both bones in my left arm. That was the end of my wrestling career, and it turned out to be the accident that redirected my life. With all the extra time on my hands, I had to find something to do, and I got a job cooking at a local pizza and ribs joint called Geppetto's.

As my friends, who weren't quite as Cro-Magnon as I, went off to good colleges I couldn't get into, I felt lost. My boss at Geppetto's said, "You want to be a chef, go to chef school."

Remember, this was 1987, and being a chef wasn't seen as glamorous. There was no Food Network, and the term "celebrity chef" didn't exist. I was essentially telling my dad I wanted to be a tradesman (which I still consider myself to be and am very proud to be). After begging, and enlisting Mom's help in convincing him, I finally got him to agree. When I hit those kitchens, I finally knew what I wanted to do with my life. I would live to cook.

KEFTEDES (MOM'S LITTLE MEATBALLS)

In Greek these babies are called *keftedes,* a word that roughly translates as "fritters." To me they are all about family and sharing and eating together—the forces that drive me in the kitchen and what this book is all about.

In addition to this version made with lamb or beef, I also make keftedes from zucchini, tomatoes, or chickpeas. They're one of my favorite treats from my childhood and I still crave them. At family gatherings, there was always a huge pile of lamb keftedes set out as finger food, and I was only allowed so many. I would try to steal some off the table while the adults were busy cocktailing (and, of course, once I got a little older I would try to sneak some ouzo, too).

Key steps in making these as flavorful as they can be are cooking down the onion and salting it as you do, toasting your spices, and using meat that isn't too lean; ask your butcher for 25 percent fat in the mixture if you're not grinding it yourself.

recipe continued on next page

Makes 20 keftedes

Canola oil, for sautéing and pan-frying
½ cup minced or grated onion
Kosher salt
1 garlic clove, smashed beneath the flat
    side of a knife and coarsely chopped
½ cup diced day-old bread
½ cup whole milk
1 pound ground beef or lamb
1 large egg
1 teaspoon torn fresh oregano leaves

¼ teaspoon ground coriander
¼ teaspoon ground cumin
⅛ teaspoon ground cinnamon
Pinch of grated nutmeg
Freshly ground black pepper
All-purpose flour, for dusting
Handful of fresh mint leaves, for serving
2 lemons, one cut into wedges
¼ cup extra-virgin olive oil

Heat 2 teaspoons of the canola oil in a medium sauté pan or skillet over medium heat. Add the onion and a three-finger pinch of salt and cook until the onion begins to release some moisture and soften, 1 or 2 minutes. Toss in the garlic and cook, stirring, until the onion is translucent and the garlic is softened, 2 or 3 minutes. Scrape out onto a plate and let cool.

Meanwhile, put the bread in a small bowl and pour in the milk.

In a mixing bowl, combine the onion and garlic and meat. Add the egg. Squeeze out the bread, discarding the milk, and add the bread along with the oregano, coriander, cumin, cinnamon, nutmeg, and a good teaspoon of pepper. Mix the ingredients with your hands until they're all evenly distributed. I like to taste this mixture raw to check for seasoning (it's delicious), but you can sauté it first if you wish. Cover with plastic wrap and refrigerate until ready to use (up to 1 day).

Form the mixture into balls, a little smaller than golf balls. You should have about 20. Roll them in flour, shaking off any excess.

In a large shallow pan, add enough canola oil to come up to about a third the height of a keftede and heat over medium heat until hot (the keftedes should sizzle immediately upon hitting the oil). Pan-fry the keftedes, turning once, until just cooked through but still moist inside and with a nice crust outside, about 5 minutes (cut open if you're unsure whether they're done). Remove to a paper-towel-lined plate to drain.

Arrange the keftedes on a serving platter. Grind some fresh pepper over them, tear mint leaves onto them, grate the zest from the whole lemon onto them, and give them a drizzle of extra-virgin olive oil and a sprinkle of salt. Serve the lemon wedges on the side for squeezing on top.

About the Chef

By Michael Ruhlman

A bell went off in my head when she said it. She was a cook at Michael Symon's Lola, the most popular restaurant in Cleveland, working day prep and I was beside her as part of my reporting on Michael Symon for my book *The Soul of a Chef*. We roasted and peeled beets and red peppers, made the chocolate pudding, washed the arugula, sliced the red onions, grilled the portobellos, and prepped the artichokes.

She stopped moving and said, "You know what I like about Michael's food? It's the kind of food you can do at home." She paused for an example but needed to go only as far as her countertop, to the artichokes, for her favorite dish: grilled halibut over a roasted artichoke salad with red peppers, basil vinaigrette, and preserved lemon. "I would *never* have thought to put halibut on an artichoke salad," she said.

I thought, "Do-at-home food—exactly. That's it."

Symon's food was interesting and satisfying and reliant on good technique, but in the end it was very simple food without pretension or self-conscious chefiness. A piece of fish over a salad, or with a little salad on top and a warm vinaigrette. Corn crêpes with some shredded duck inside and a little barbecue sauce. A chicken dish that was so successful he grew to despise it: he couldn't take it off the menu because women threatened never to come back if he did. Rigatoni pasta tossed in a cream sauce flavored with rosemary and goat cheese (see page 89); if you have some leftover chicken, a one-dish meal comes together in the time it takes the rigatoni to cook. Anyone can do it, there is almost no technique whatsoever, and yet it is good enough to earn national accolades from the food media. This guy, this wrestler, this blue-collar boy from Cleveland . . . a *Food & Wine* best-chef award? Really?

I'd known Symon for a couple years before he sprang onto the national playing field. I had spent some time in the kitchen at his previous restaurant, but after the award in 1998 I could write about him for a broader audience. What was it about this guy that was so magnetic? What made his food both so good and also so seemingly simple?

One of the qualities of his dishes is their mechanical ingenuity, born of necessity in the chaotic bottom-line restaurant business. When you have nothing more than a shoebox kitchen and a six-burner range to feed two hundred people, you're forced to think a little harder. The aforementioned pasta dish needs only one pan to come together. ("If I can't finish a dish in two pans, I won't do it," Symon always says, summing up his hot-line philosophy.) Very few of his dishes rely on elaborate reductions; he uses hardly any stocks at all. Give him a warm vinaigrette over a gluey veal-stock reduction any day. His cooking is focused.

I remember eating at the bar one night after I'd finished my scribbling. I liked to rib Symon about how little sauce he used. I'd say, "Sorry, Michael, I just don't like dry food." And he'd say, "Yeah, but I sell more wine this way!" And he'd howl and keep cooking.

I ordered the brick-roasted chicken. He hadn't used any sauce, it seemed, and he hadn't used any stock. Half a roasted chicken stuffed with seared hen-of-the-woods mushrooms that came straight out of the broiler was placed on a mound of red potatoes sautéed with arugula, some cream, and some mustard. The "finish the dish in two pans or fewer" rule.

Michael threw some cooked red potatoes into a sauté pan, followed by a handful of arugula. The greens released some of their liquid. He then added a little cream to the pan, which helped to heat up the potatoes and sweeten the spicy greens, and a spoonful of mustard for acidity, balance. When the chicken came out of the broiler, he poured the creamy potato-arugula side dish onto a plate, set the chicken right on top of that, and let it rest there for a few minutes. As it rested, the chicken dropped its natural juices and mushroom juices over the potatoes and into the mustard cream, creating an extraordinary and complex sauce all on its own. It was a kind of self-saucing dish. No one had to toil over a classic stock or make a pan jus or even ladle sauce out of a nearby bain-marie. The dish was making its own sauce right there and all he needed was to squirt a few drops of balsamic to finish it. Ingenious. Try it yourself (see page 198). This is how he could turn tables four times on a Saturday night and not keep losing his line cooks.

Symon's food isn't simplistic; it is just simple and economical, the two main criteria for home cooking. Another reason his placement on *Food & Wine*'s 1998 best-new-chefs list was remarkable was the price point his restaurant had to hit. His market is a meat-and-potatoes crowd unwilling to pay New York City prices and suspicious of anyone trying to charge them. The nine other chefs on the *Food & Wine* list had white-tablecloth dining rooms serving expensive ingredients at high prices, the kind of ingredients that tend to impress foodie magazines but have a high food cost. These chefs had check averages that ranged from $70 to $150.

Hanging out at Lola early one evening, I saw a man and a woman, both dressed in fine business attire, approach the bar for an after-dinner drink. Bartender Frankie Ritz (now managing the Detroit restaurant—another reason for Symon's success: he takes care of people and they stay with him), polishing a glass, with a ready smile asked, "How was your meal?" The man swirled his Cognac and said, "I had the halibut. It was out of this world. Most expensive thing on the menu. Nineteen ninety-five. 'Gimme the most expensive thing on the menu.' *Nineteen ninety-five.*" The man chuckled and shook his head. Evidently one of those New York City types we get around here every now and then.

Michael Symon knew his market and in 1998, he wouldn't put an entrée on the menu for more than twenty dollars. Symon earned a best-new-chef award by doing thirty-dollar check averages per person. *That's* what was amazing. He'd become one of the best chefs in the country by serving do-at-home food. Symon was so successful, when a developer needed an anchor for an entire street redevelopment project, he called on Michael. Michael shut down Lola to rebuild it on the new street in downtown Cleveland and reopened the original restaurant as Lolita.

I loved hanging out at the restaurant because it was so easy to be there, the atmosphere was so light. During the day, prep was casual and laughter was continual. When service began at five, the room seemed simply to fill up with more friends. I'd sometimes be surprised to find Chatty Matty, Matt Harlan—now chef de cuisine of Lolita—putting up the first courses, only to look around and realize that the people at the tables were customers and not just friends coming to hang out. I think that's another reason for Symon's success. He, and critically his wife, Liz, create places that are fun to be in. You're always glad to be there. It's like a family. I loved reporting from both restaurants because they were a pleasure just to be a part of the family for a while. The places were filled with smiles—and they had the same effect on the rest of Cleveland as they had on me. People felt like they were part of the family.

All of which is why I'm so excited about this book. I knew Michael would create an uncompromising chef's book that speaks directly to home cooks without talking down to chefs or simplifying any of the food. This is not four-star cooking at home, at home with the four-star chef. His food is simple and ingenious. It has an excitement generated from thoughtful flavor pairings, an integrity based on Michael's Mediterranean–Eastern European heritage and his twenty-plus-year commitment to food and cooking and the restaurant business. Michael is true to who he is and where he comes from—from Cleveland, a city defined by simplicity, ethnic diversity, economical thrift, hearty fare, and a distaste for pretension.

But most of all, he makes the food fun. It's the kind of food that, when you see him cooking it, or even listen to him talking about it, makes you want to go home and do it yourself. He makes cooking fun.

Becoming a Better Cook

I think all chefs, at least on some level, want their own cookbook, a record of their work, not for posterity but rather, on some level, for permanence, because what we do nightly disappears faster than it takes to create it. Our work, if it's any good, vanishes and the better it is, the faster it goes away! On the other hand, I have never wanted simply a collection of recipes. Recipes are important but only to a point. What's more important than recipes is how we think about food, and a good cookbook should open up a new way of doing just that. My favorite cookbooks (page 222) are those that have changed the way I think about food and cooking. My goal in *Live to Cook* is to make great food more approachable for home cooks and to do so without dumbing down or simplifying the food or the cooking.

My cooking and this book are above all about approachable food, food that isn't heavily fussed over; food that is what it is and tastes delicious. It's how my food has always been at my restaurants, how my food is at home. And I think approachability is what chefs need to keep in mind when they share their food with the home cook. The food I've been doing my whole career is straightforward: there's no masking of flavors, and the dishes are economical and efficient, with minimal embellishments, but with big, big flavors and soulful satisfactions.

In the end, great food is nothing more than this: great ingredients, sound technique. That's all there is to it. To become a better cook, always be thinking about those two things, always be asking yourself, are my ingredients excellent and am I applying good techniques to what I have?

Do you want to know how to improve your cooking? The first thing you can do, and you can start doing this immediately, is start shopping better. That is the number-one way to become a better cook: buy better ingredients. For produce, buy with the seasons—that is, buy what grows naturally in that season. Don't try to buy a decent tomato in January; buy them in the summer. Peas and asparagus in the spring. Citrus fruits in the late winter. Buy fresh oils, good vinegars. You get what you pay for here: the range of quality is broad in oils and vinegars and other condiments. Pay for them and use them well. The excellent-quality ingredients are not that much more expensive than the cheap stuff, and odds are, if you pay a little more money for a good balsamic or a good sherry vinegar, you're less likely to waste it. If you buy a gorgeous piece of fish, you're going to take care of it and pay attention to cooking it well.

The second way to improve your cooking is to master fundamental techniques, those techniques that span all of cooking. I'm not talking about fancy knife skills or

anything showy. Just the basics. First and foremost, learn how to use salt, how to season your food, and, more important, *when* to season it (see page 23). Learn how hot to get your pan; make sure your fat gets hot enough before you put the food in the pan. Sweating vegetables—cooking them down without browning them—is a critical facet of cooking and has a huge impact on the depth of flavor of a finished dish. These are not optional details but the very backbone of the preparation. Pay attention to these early steps, these fundamental techniques, which are discussed in special sections throughout the book, and your cooking will grow better every day.

I cook at my restaurants the way I cook at home—using excellent ingredients and solid technique—and whether it's crispy sweetbreads or Mom's pot roast, the ingredients are treated with the same respect. And that's what's in this book. Straightforward recipes for the food I make at my restaurants and the food I cook at home. Nothing is very difficult. Some dishes do take a little more time or involve a few more steps. Some require hands-on commitment from the cook, such as the risotto and the pierogies, and others you can do in between beers on the patio with your buddies. Some of the recipes feature ingredients that might not be standard in your local grocery store, such as beef and pork cheeks. I offer substitutions wherever I can, but you should know that these ingredients are available; grocery stores are becoming more willing to source ingredients for you if you ask them to. And there's literally nothing that I can get that you can't via suppliers in your city or via the Internet, which is a great resource for the home cook.

I think side dishes are undervalued in cookbooks, yet they're so important at home. How often do we make complete composed plates for our families? Side dishes are so much fun, and so easy, that I almost opened the book with them. I sometimes think of what sides I feel like eating and throw a piece of quickly cooked meat in there for some substance. Next time you plan a meal, don't start by deciding what the main dish is, a sirloin steak or side of salmon; instead, find a side dish that you like, braised endive or peas and pancetta—whatever looks great at the market—and build the meal around that. This is how we eat at home, how I cook at home. The composed plate is for the restaurant chef, and the only dishes I've presented in the book as complete plates are the fish entrées, because I think certain fish go really well with the side components I've suggested.

Otherwise the main courses are by themselves, though I'll often suggest some sides for them. And the other main courses are served family style, because that's my favorite way to eat: big platters of food for all to share.

I'm also excited by a few special sections in this book. First charcuterie, one of the most important branches of cooking there is—the one having to do with preservation, originally, but which we now practice because the flavors are so good: sausages, bacon, confit. I was almost surprised to find a whole pickling section develop as we created this book. I know I love pickles, but I didn't realize how pervasive they are in my cooking. I use them all over, and in different ways, and I employ different pickling techniques. It's yet another simple way to improve your cooking—to understand what powerful tools acid and crunch are. And the final special section is devoted to prepared sauces, which give you flexibility and versatility in the kitchen.

Shop Better

All food is not created equal. I repeat: *The easiest way to improve your food is to improve how you shop.* No matter how good a cook or chef you are, if you start with garbage you will end up with garbage. It's that simple.

Look for food that's natural, meaning not processed—which usually means it doesn't come in a box or bag or, if it does, it contains only three or four ingredients. Choose food that's organic, and whenever possible, produced near where you live.

Be aware of what's in season. This will not only save you money but it will also help you avoid eating a tomato that tastes like cardboard, which is what you'll taste when you eat tomatoes in the middle of winter in Cleveland. If you're lucky enough to have farmers' markets in your area they are a great place to start, as you can often meet the farmers who are producing your food. Talk to them about its variety and how it was raised or grown. It's odd to me that people will put endless hours into researching the car they are going to buy but could not care less about where the chicken they feed to their family comes from! Know your source. It gives you a much better appreciation of what you are eating.

If you search out heirloom and heritage items, you will quickly realize the flavor differences within a specific product or breed. Choose the ones you enjoy the most.

Avoid the evil empires of food, the companies that mass-produce cheap products. Their food tastes insipid, it is not good for you, and it is worse for the animal, the land, the farmer, and the environment involved. If you can buy food, toilet paper, toys for your kids, and a lawnmower all at the same place, it is time to change your food shopping habits.

Five Things You Should Never Buy

1. **Boneless, skinless chicken breast halves.** Eating chicken without skin is like riding a bike without wheels: it's no fun, and it leaves your dish at a flavor standstill.
2. **Lean turkey bacon.** There is no substitute for the magic that is smoky, fatty, delicious bacon, and the word *lean* should never be used when describing it.
3. **I Can't Believe It's Not Butter! and other butter substitutes.** Believe me, it *ain't* butter, not even close. I'm certain the people who invented this have never really tasted butter and have never tried to make a sauce with it. Stay away from margarine, too. The only thing to use to replace butter is more butter.
4. **Beef tenderloin/filet mignon.** Can we please get over our love affair with the most expensive and least flavorful part of the entire animal? Buy a beautifully marbled rib eye; it'll cost you less and make you happier.
5. **Peeled, chopped garlic.** The only thing that this has in common with fresh garlic is the breath it may produce. It certainly lacks the actual flavor of garlic. Are we really so lazy that we have to buy our garlic already cut for us?

On Salt

Learning to use salt well is one of the biggest steps you can take in becoming a better cook. I can't stress enough the importance of salt; it is without a shadow of a doubt the most critical ingredient in your kitchen. It's what makes food come alive and brings out all the flavors. Without it, great food simply is not possible. One of the best examples of its powerful effect is on a tomato. This summer, slice a fresh local tomato. Taste it. Now sprinkle some kosher salt on a slice and taste this, and you will sense the difference. Salt not only pulls out the flavor of the tomato but also helps open your palate to accept the flavor. Salt has that kind of impact throughout your cooking, from savory to sweet. If you feel that the unsalted tomato tastes better, you should go see a doctor, because something is seriously wrong with your taste buds.

There are different ways to salt your food and different times to do it, each producing a specific result. When building a soup or sauce, make sure you salt as you go, seasoning onion, carrots, celery, and other ingredients while they are sweating; this will bring out their full flavor and sweetness, which will give you the best results. By the time the sauce or soup is done, it should be fully seasoned. You may need to add a pinch or so at the end, but if you need a ton you dropped the ball and lost out on flavor.

Opinion varies widely on when to salt meat and fish. I've tried every way imaginable and here's what I found works best. With meats, game, and fowl, I salt anywhere between eight and twenty-four hours—removing the meat from the refrigerator for twenty to sixty minutes, depending on its size—before I cook it. This is also a great time to add any other seasonings—herbs or spices—to the meat, as the salt helps the flavor penetrate the muscle. This might contradict whatever you've heard, but trust me, it works. I didn't believe it myself, but several years ago two of my chefs at Lolita, Jonathon Sawyer and Jon Seeholzer, told me they wanted to try presalting the meat. After much debate and arguing over why it would or wouldn't work, I suggested we do a side-by-side taste test. To my surprise, the presalted chop not only tasted better, but it was also juicier.

I salt seafood right before it goes into the heat. Although I enjoy the flavor that pre-salting gives to fish, it tends to firm up the flesh and I don't like the texture.

For vegetables that are about to be grilled or sautéed, I like to salt about thirty minutes in advance to pull out any additional liquid or bitterness in the vegetable. This will really make your vegetables sing and bring out all their sweetness and flavor.

It should go without saying, but I'll say it, just in case: avoid iodized table salt. It has an acrid chemical flavor, and as long as you have a varied diet, you won't need the iodide supplement. I use coarse kosher salt for most seasoning. I prefer Diamond Crystal for its feel—we almost always measure with our fingers and you can get a great sense of just how much you're adding—and because it doesn't have the anti-caking agents Morton's does. I use a coarse sea salt or *fleur de sel*, a very special, light flavorful salt from Brittany, for finishing dishes. It adds a delicate salty crunch.

Creating and Building Your Own Dishes: The Elements of Balance

Once you have shopped for and brought home excellent ingredients, you'll need a game plan for putting them together.

There are many theories and thoughts that go into creating a good dish. Most chefs and home cooks will have opinions on what makes one dish great and what causes another to falter. Assuming you have seasoned everything properly—meaning the right amount at the right time—the most important quality in a dish is balance.

When a dish fails, it's usually not because the flavors are bad, but rather because the flavors and textures are not balanced. Often chefs will have a dish that's all fat, or all soft—with no crunch or crisp. Braised short ribs with mashed potatoes: fat on fat, soft on soft. I find that tragic. But it can be fixed by adding components that are crisp, bright, and acidic. Serve those braised short ribs with some root vegetables and a gremolata, or with an herb salad tossed in a vinaigrette, and the dish begins to find some balance and brightness.

To create a dish, I'll often write down a list of proteins in one column and a list of seasonal vegetables and fruits in another. I'll tend toward rich, braised dishes in the cold months and lighter, more tender items that are sautéed or grilled in the summer.

If the central item is rich, I begin to think how to balance the richness with acidic and bitter components. If it's lean, I think about how to balance that protein with fat. Halibut is a lean fish, so if that were the central item, I'd first think about what fat would go with it—some butter, or cream, or bacon, say. And once I had the fat, I'd think about the acidic component to balance that. I might grill or sauté that halibut in the summer, serve it with heirloom tomatoes for their sweetness and acidity, add some Ohio sweet corn, and maybe flavor the corn with cream and bacon.

Without question two of the most critical elements of a dish are fat and acid. The fat is what gives you that great mouthfeel and helps satisfy your soul. Whether the fat comes from a butter or cream or from the protein itself, it's this richness that makes food fulfilling.

The acidity helps cut through the fat as you're eating and keeps your palate alive and jumping. There are many ways to add acidity to a dish. Splash some vinegar into a braising liquid, add citrus to a butter sauce, or top a steak with pickled vegetables. Of course there's always the squeeze of lemon, which is easy, complements almost any food, and is excellent with all things fried. Acidity, like salt, also helps to open up your palate and accept the flavors.

And finally, varying textures are critical to the success of a dish. These can be established in many different ways: Add crispy fried pork cracklings to a salad; add crunchy lettuces or vegetables to soft braises. The Slash-and-Burn Grouper (page 175) is soft and delicate so I knew I wanted a crunchy garnish: crispy Crab Tater Tots (page 165). Always consider the textures in a dish and make sure you have contrasts.

Two final qualities of a dish's composition are spicy and bitter. Bitter, like acid, can create a great counterpoint to richness. I use different lettuces, such as endive or radicchio, because they not only give that great flavor contrast to the dish, they also add texture and temperature contrast. A great example of this is garnishing a rich hanger steak with some lightly dressed arugula. When eaten together the sharp arugula will help cut through the bloody richness of the steak and give the dish some crunch.

Spice can be a tricky thing. What one person finds mild another may find nuclear. There are some ways to balance the heat so you can coax the depth of the flavor from a chile and not just be hit with raw heat. I am a huge fan of pickling chilies for that reason: pickling helps balance the heat with the addition of sugar and vinegar (see page 120). To me, spicy just for the sake of spicy is ridiculous. When used correctly, spice can help create great contrasts and flavors and really make food come alive. Just remember that heat does vary from chile to chile—one jalapeño can be fiery and the next one relatively mild—so tasting is the key. Also remember that most of the heat is in the ribs and seeds, which can be removed to temper their heat.

The following dish is an illustration of the simplicity and balance I'm trying to describe here, the sweetness of the fish, the sweet acidity of the lemon, the salty acidity of the caperberries, and the nuttiness and crunch from the almonds—all tied together with a simple butter, olive oil, and lemon sauce.

SLOW-ROASTED HALIBUT WITH FRIED CAPERS, CARAMELIZED LEMON, AND ALMONDS

Halibut can be a tricky fish to cook because it is so lean, especially Pacific halibut, which is what I recommend for sustainability reasons. Cooking it in a slow oven makes it harder to overcook the fish and helps maintain the delicate flavor of the halibut, which you can lose if you use very high heat. Also, I think halibut is a fish that should be cooked through, not well, but not medium-rare either; an internal temperature of 130° to 140°F is perfect.

I pair the halibut with a very easy butter sauce: seared lemon slices sautéed with crunchy sliced almonds, briny caperberries, and shallots and finished with garlic and parsley. It's a classic quick Greek sauce, in essence. Sometimes I'll add a tablespoon of chopped anchovies as well to give it another dimension of salty savoriness. I love the caramelized lemon: the heat releases its juices and seasons the sauce with a little sweetness. You can treat any citrus fruit this way.

Serves 4

4 halibut fillets, 6 to 8 ounces each, skin removed
Kosher salt
2 tablespoons extra-virgin olive oil
3 tablespoons unsalted butter
4 (¼-inch-thick) slices lemon

¼ cup sliced almonds
5 large caperberries, halved lengthwise
¼ cup thinly sliced shallots
1½ tablespoons thinly sliced garlic
½ cup sliced flat-leaf parsley

Preheat the oven to 225°F.

Season the halibut fillets on both sides with salt. In a cold nonstick, ovenproof sauté pan that can hold all four fillets, pour in 1 tablespoon of the olive oil. Put the fish in the pan and rub the top of the fillets with the remaining 1 tablespoon olive oil. Slide the pan into the oven and cook the fish until it reaches an internal temperature of 130° to 140°F and flakes easily when prodded with a fork, 12 to 15 minutes.

A few minutes after you put the fish in the oven, heat 1 tablespoon of the butter in a medium saucepan over high heat. When the butter is hot and foaming, add the lemon slices and cook them until they begin to caramelize, 2 to 3 minutes. Flip the lemons, add the sliced almonds and caperberries, and sauté for 30 seconds. Add the shallots and sauté for another 30 seconds. Add the garlic, parsley, and the remaining 2 tablespoons butter. Continue to cook until the lemons soften and the almonds and butter brown, about 2 minutes.

Place the halibut fillets on warm plates or a warm serving platter and spoon the capers, lemon, almonds, and butter sauce over them.

Starters

The following recipes are all great small dishes to open a meal; many of them are also terrific as hors d'oeuvres if you're having people over. These dishes range from incredibly simple to moderately time consuming, though none are difficult. The dates and the tuna are super easy. The crispy pig's ears and pierogies require a few steps but are worth the effort. What I love most about this selection of recipes, though, is that it represents my whole life as a cook. I've been eating and making fritters and stuffed peppers since my childhood, the pierogies have been a restaurant staple for years, and it's only in the past few years that I've fallen in love with pig's ears, so these simple dishes show the entire range of my life as cook.

ROASTED DATES WITH PANCETTA, ALMONDS, AND CHILE

These are incredibly simple—sliced almonds and red pepper flakes are added to sautéing pancetta and then spooned over roasted dates—but so addictive. The beauty of this preparation is the intensity and concentration of all the flavors: the sweetness of the dates, but also the savory saltiness of the pancetta, nuttiness of the almonds, and spicy heat of the chile. It's the perfect balance of the taste elements I love. Your mouth will just pop with these flavors.

At Players restaurant, my first restaurant after culinary school, chef-owner Mark Shary used to stuff a date with an almond, wrap it in bacon, and roast it. These morsels were served on toothpicks. This is my interpretation, turning a little snack or hors d'oeuvre into a bona fide starter. Leftover dates can be puréed and used as a spread on croutons or served as a condiment with a cheese course.

Serves 4 to 6

2 cups pitted dates
3 ounces pancetta, finely diced (½ cup)
½ cup sliced almonds
1 teaspoon minced garlic
1 teaspoon crushed red pepper flakes

1 cup Chicken Stock (page 131)
1 tablespoon unsalted butter
1 tablespoon fresh lemon juice
1 tablespoon chopped fresh flat-leaf
 parsley leaves

Preheat the oven to 350°F.

Put the dates on a small rimmed baking sheet and roast in the oven until heated through, about 5 minutes. Turn off the oven but leave the dates in there while you cook the pancetta.

In a medium sauté pan over medium heat, cook the pancetta until it is three-quarters crisp, about 5 minutes. Add the almonds and continue cooking until they brown, a few minutes. Add the garlic and cook for another minute or so. Add the red pepper flakes and stock and bring to a simmer, scraping the bottom of the pan with a wooden spoon. Remove the pan from the heat and whisk in the butter, stirring continuously until the butter is melted. Stir in the lemon juice and parsley.

Add the dates to the pan and swirl and toss them in the sauce. Divide the cooked dates among four to six plates and spoon the sauce over them.

SPICY STUFFED PEPPERS

Hot peppers from my yia yia's garden, grilled outside, were a staple of my childhood. We grew what we called Hungarian hots, also known as Hungarian wax peppers or banana peppers—long, pale green or yellow tapering peppers. Some years the peppers would be smoking hot and other years they'd be mild; we never knew why, but the not knowing was always part of the fun. (These are also the peppers used in Shasha Sauce, page 138.) Sometimes we'd simply throw them on the grill. Here I stuff them. It's a fantastic way to use loose sausage, and I like the shape of these particular peppers for stuffing. Bell peppers are really too big for this kind of grilled preparation, but poblanos would also be excellent.

Serves 4 to 8

8 Hungarian hot peppers
1½ pounds Pork Sausage (page 103) or
   Italian sausage (see Symon Says)

2 cups Yia Yia's Sunday Sauce (page 229)
   or jarred tomato sauce
8 fresh basil leaves

Preheat the oven to 375°F. Light coals in a charcoal grill for a medium-hot fire. Butter an 8 by 11-inch baking dish.

Cut the tops off of the peppers and spoon out any seeds. Divide the sausage into 8 equal portions and spoon it into the peppers to fill them.

Pour the sauce into the prepared baking dish.

Grill the peppers to char them on the outside, about 2 minutes per side. Remove them from the grill and lay the peppers on top of the sauce. Bake for 10 minutes, or until the sausage reaches an internal temperature of 150°F. Divide among plates, spoon some tomato sauce on top, and garnish each with a basil leaf.

SYMON SAYS

Although it is best to make your own sausage, if you're pinched for time, butcher shops and many grocery stores such as Whole Foods offer an array of fresh sausage. If only good link sausage is available, remove the casing and use the loose sausage.

If you don't want to heat your grill *and* your oven, you can do all of this in the oven: preheat the broiler and char the peppers underneath the broiler. Remove them from the oven, reduce the oven temperature to 375°F, and proceed with the recipe.

LAMB TARTARE WITH LEMON AND GREEK YOGURT

In July 2007, in the kitchens of the Culinary Institute of America, eight of us had twenty minutes to make a dish to be judged by each other in a reality television cooking show called *Next Iron Chef America*. I chose lamb and because of the time constraints decided on a tartare, a spin on classic beef tartare. Tartare is simply raw meat, diced or ground, and seasoned with what amounts to a vinaigrette. Here it was lemon juice, olive oil, and yogurt, and for even more flavor, mint, cilantro, coriander, and olives. My tartare was the winning dish, which really got my momentum going in the contest; it was especially gratifying to be so honored by my peers (as opposed to the snarky, know-nothing judges!).

I love the brininess of the olives, which pair perfectly with the gaminess of the lamb. My favorites for cooking are oil-cured Moroccan olives, followed by briny green picholines, black kalamatas, and green lucques.

The key elements to preparing this dish are keeping everything cold, and making sure not to add the lemon juice until the last possible minute; if added too far in advance, it will in effect cook the meat and alter its texture. Raw lamb is fine to eat, provided it's handled properly. I recommend you buy a whole cut of meat, rinse and dry it well, and dice it yourself.

Serves 4 to 6

1 pound lamb loin or sirloin, finely diced
1 teaspoon chopped fresh mint
1 teaspoon chopped fresh cilantro
¼ teaspoon ground coriander
2 tablespoons chopped olives
1 tablespoon minced shallot

1 tablespoon extra-virgin olive oil
1 teaspoon kosher salt
1 teaspoon freshly ground black pepper
Grated zest and juice of 1 lemon
4 to 6 tablespoons Greek yogurt

Combine the lamb, mint, cilantro, coriander, olives, shallot, olive oil, salt, pepper, and lemon zest in a nonreactive bowl and mix thoroughly. This can be done up to several hours before serving and refrigerated. Add the lemon juice just before serving. Divide the lamb among four to six plates and garnish each serving with a tablespoon of yogurt.

ZUCCHINI FRITTERS WITH FETA AND DILL

In Greece, fritters are called *keftedes* and they vary from island to island and with the season. Keftedes can be made with tomatoes, chickpeas, or even with ground meat, like the ones my mom serves at family gatherings (page 11). Zucchini is a great vegetable for keftedes. I grate the entire thing, seeds and all, salt it, wring it out, and then make the fritters. These keftedes can be served as an hors d'oeuvre or a starter course and they don't even need a sauce; just sprinkle some salt and crumbled feta on top.

Makes about 8 fritters; serves 4

2 medium zucchini
1 teaspoon kosher salt
1 tablespoon chopped fresh mint
1½ tablespoons chopped fresh dill, plus whole dill for garnish
1 large scallion, white and green parts, thinly sliced on the bias
2 teaspoons minced garlic
¼ teaspoon freshly ground black pepper

4 ounces feta cheese, coarsely chopped or crumbled
Grated zest of 1 lemon
1 large egg
3 tablespoons all-purpose flour
Canola oil, for pan-frying
½ cup Greek yogurt
Coarse sea salt, for garnish

Grate the zucchini on the large holes of a grater onto a clean kitchen towel. Sprinkle with the kosher salt and let it rest while you gather and prep the remaining ingredients.

Wrap the zucchini in the towel and wring as much liquid out of it as possible, discarding the liquid. In a medium bowl, combine the zucchini, mint, dill, scallion, garlic, pepper, feta, and all but 1 teaspoon of the lemon zest. Stir in the egg and flour and mix until well combined.

Add the canola oil to a large shallow pan; you want about ¼ inch or enough so that when all the fritters are in the pan, the oil comes halfway up their sides. Place the pan over medium-high heat. Form fritters by hand or using a ¼-cup measure, and fry them in the hot oil in batches. Cook until the fritters are golden brown on each side, 4 to 6 minutes. Drain on paper towels.

Transfer the fritters to plates and garnish with a dollop of Greek yogurt and a sprinkling of dill, the reserved lemon zest, and some coarse sea salt.

LIGHTLY CURED TUNA WITH OLIVES, ORANGE, AND SHAVED FENNEL

This dish is based on the ancient Greek preparation called *spinialo*. Fishermen would travel down from their homes in the mountains to head out to sea for several weeks. For the journey home, they would take some of the fish they had caught, cut it into cubes, put it into empty wine jugs, and fill the bottles with sea water. The salt in the water would cure the fish. They would then eat the fish with a squeeze of lemon and some wild herbs, which would sustain them during their journey home.

I cure the fish with the brine from the olives, which imparts a mild olive flavor. Here I use cerignola, which I love in raw preparations, but you could use kalamata, niçoise, or any other black, brine-cured olive. You need to leave the fish in the brine for at least thirty minutes—the tuna picks up flavors fast. Depending how far you want to take it, though, you could leave the tuna in the cure for up to a day. To keep the fishermen's tradition, we serve it with some freshly shaved fennel and fennel fronds, which grow wild in Greece (though some pickled fennel would also be delicious), along with a squeeze of orange juice and a drizzle of extra-virgin olive oil.

Serves 4

½ pound sushi-grade tuna loin
10 cerignola olives, pitted and left whole,
     with ¾ cup olive brine, or more if
     needed to cover the fish slices
1 large orange, segmented (see Symon
     Says, page 73), juice reserved

2 tablespoons chopped fennel fronds
Freshly ground black pepper
½ small bulb fennel, shaved (½ cup)
Fresh cilantro leaves, for garnish
Extra-virgin olive oil, for garnish
Coarse sea salt, for garnish

Slice the tuna across the grain into ¼-inch-thick slices. Lay the slices in a deep glass or ceramic dish, pour in enough olive brine just to cover the fish, and let it cure for at least 30 minutes (or refrigerate, covered, for up to a day). Add the olives, reserved orange juice, and fennel fronds. Grind fresh black pepper over each slice of fish.

To serve, divide the fish among four shallow bowls and top with the orange segments and shaved fennel, olives, and some of the curing juices. Garnish each serving with a few cilantro leaves, a drizzle of extra-virgin olive oil, and a sprinkling of coarse sea salt.

Starting Out

When I graduated from the CIA in 1990, I wanted to return to my hometown and family. I'd cooked at various restaurants in New York, which was exciting, but the things that mattered most to me were in Cleveland.

The key, I knew then, was to be humble and take the job that would teach me the most, not the one that paid the most. But I knew I had to stay focused and keep my eye on the prize, which was to one day own my own restaurant. It was then, and still is, all about the food.

After searching for weeks in Cleveland for the right fit, I landed a job at a restaurant called Players, in a close-in suburb on the west side of Cleveland, under chef-owner Mark Shary. I talked to chefs all over the city and Mark was really the only one, in 1990, who I felt was truly one hundred percent passionate about food. Even though he was a completely self-taught chef, his passion was just so evident, so obvious, that I knew I wanted to work for him. And a few things happened at Players that were critical to my development as a cook—moments of understanding that are important for any cook to go through.

It was at this restaurant that I first learned how to salt food. Mark taught me not only how but, more important, when. If you're making a sauce or any preparation that involves sweating aromatic vegetables—cooking onions and garlic until they're translucent but not brown, one of the most common techniques in the kitchen—salt them immediately; don't wait until all your ingredients are in the pot. Salt your vegetables as they sweat.

It was from Mark that I learned—saw, tasted—the importance of roasting food on the bone, whether it's chicken, fish, or a short rib. It's the best way of cooking the food evenly and keeping it juicy and flavorful. Mark taught me the finer points of braising—the importance, for example, of infusing a stock with additional aromatics before the seared meat goes into it. These may seem like small issues, but it's these details that, when they all come together, make the difference between good cooking and great cooking.

There was no such thing as a good shortcut for Mark. We would go through ten gallons of roasted garlic a week and he still would absolutely refuse to buy peeled garlic, a rule I still live by. We would roast five big sheet pans of red peppers, every day, then peel and seed them rather than buy preroasted ones.

But maybe the most important thing Mark showed me was where great cooking comes from. He was a self-taught chef; he learned by traveling and reading and doing. He was a pure cook, no compromises. He showed me how to bring your soul to the food. I was a passionate person, always had been; but Mark showed me how to apply that passion to food.

CRISPY PIG'S EARS WITH PICKLED VEGETABLES

One of the amazing things about the pig is that it gives us so many different products: the belly for bacon, the shoulder for braising or smoking, scraps for sausages, the hams, the hocks, the offal. We too easily get sucked into only considering the main cuts of meat, when the entire creature is edible. After the belly, maybe my favorite part of the pig is its ears. I first had them at the Spotted Pig, a great restaurant in New York run by April Bloomfield. I had cooked and eaten pig's ears several times, but never thought much of them until Mario Batali, a partner of the restaurant (and an Iron Chef), told me to confit them first instead of braising or boiling them. That's when I truly fell in love with these crunchy morsels and knew immediately I had to serve them in Cleveland. At first they were a tough sell, but gradually word caught on and now they sell out whenever we put them on the menu at Lolita. People say, "These are what I see at the pet store—I can't believe how good these are!"

They're composed of skin and soft cartilage, which needs to be broken down, either by braising or by confiting. And this is one of the things I love about them— the long process. This is not weeknight cooking, but good things come to those who wait. To confit them, we season them first with salt and spices, and then cook them slowly in rendered fat until they're so soft you can pinch your fingers through them. They're then cooled and when we're ready to serve them, we cut them into chip-sized pieces and fry them, so they're crispy on the outside, chewy and unctuous inside. All that fat needs some nice acidity for balance, so I serve them with a salad of shaved pickled vegetables. They're also great, sliced, wherever bacon would be a traditional garnish, such as on a frisée salad or spinach salad (see page 71). Or they might be used as a textural contrast to a braised pork dish. It's hard to go wrong with these things.

Specialty butchers should be able to order them for you, or maybe even your local grocery store can do it. Another source of pig's ears may be at farmers' markets; if there's a vendor or farmer selling pork, ask if you can order ears. They should be clean and smooth, free of any bristles.

Duck fat can be bought at specialty markets or by mail from dartagnan.com, but other fats can be used as well. If lard is available, that's the next best choice, but vegetable shortening will work also, and so will olive oil. If you intend to keep them in the fat for longer periods, it's best to use a fat that is solid at room temperature.

Serves 12

12 pig's ears
3 tablespoons kosher salt
½ teaspoon ground cinnamon
4 teaspoons coriander seeds, toasted
  and ground (see Symon Says, page
  69; 1 tablespoon)
2 garlic cloves, minced

1 shallot, minced
Grated zest of 1 orange
4 cups duck fat
Canola oil, for deep-frying
¾ cup pickled vegetables
Whole-grain mustard

In a nonreactive container, toss the pig's ears with the salt, cinnamon, toasted and ground coriander, garlic, shallot, and orange zest. Cover and refrigerate for 48 hours.

Preheat the oven to 225°F.

Remove the ears from the container, rinse under cold water, and pat them dry. Combine the ears and duck fat in a 6-quart Dutch oven and cover with a lid or foil. Place in the oven and cook, undisturbed, for 14 hours. Remove from the oven and let the ears cool submerged in the fat. Store in the refrigerator until ready to serve, or up to 1 month.

Pour enough oil into a medium pot so that the oil comes 3 inches up the sides. Heat the oil to 375°F.

Remove the ears from the fat and cut them into quarters. Fry until crisp, about 4 minutes. Serve accompanied by pickled vegetables and whole-grain mustard.

SYMON SAYS
Moisture can get trapped within the skin and it is sometimes released with a pop, so it's a good idea to cover the pot with a splatter guard while frying these.

CORN CRÊPES WITH BARBECUE DUCK CONFIT

A simple crêpe batter loaded with fresh summer corn and bright sweet bell pepper is a delicious vehicle for all kinds of ingredients. We had these on the menu at Lola for so long that every time I think of them, I think of my longtime chef, Frank Rogers. He made them by the dozen, every day, between three and five P.M. It was like having a sundial in the restaurant: when you saw Frank making the corn crêpes, you knew what time it was.

As with many dishes, this one is based on one I learned in my early years with Mark Shary. Then, at Players, we would fill them with chorizo and top them off with sour cream, an excellent dish. Here I opt for the glory of duck confit, seasoned with some coffee barbecue sauce. Confit keeps for weeks well covered and stored in the fridge, and these crêpes freeze beautifully (separate them with layers of parchment, and wrap in plastic), so this is a dish that can be prepared days or weeks in advance of a special occasion or simply to have around for a last-minute appetizer or light meal.

I like to let this batter rest for a couple of hours to allow the flour to bloom, or hydrate. These are a special summer treat if you wait for the good corn. And, again, these won't only work with duck confit; turn leftovers into a new meal by replacing the confit with shredded or diced chicken or pot roast, opting for the same barbecue sauce or for tomato sauce (see page 229). They'd be excellent filled with pulled pork. Vegetarian is not something I often strive for, but these could be rolled around goat cheese, or stuffed with a good ricotta mixed with lime zest or sautéed spinach.

Serves 4

Crêpe Batter

½ cup fresh or thawed, frozen corn kernels

½ cup all-purpose flour

2 large eggs

½ cup whole milk

¼ teaspoon kosher salt

Freshly ground black pepper

½ cup coarsely chopped cored and seeded red bell pepper

½ cup coarsely chopped cored and seeded green bell pepper

¼ cup coarsely chopped scallion, white and green parts

Canola oil, for sautéing

Barbecue Duck Confit

1 cup shredded Duck Confit (page 110) or filling of your choice

1 cup Coffee Barbecue Sauce (page 135)

½ cup sour cream

Combine the corn, flour, eggs, milk, salt, pepper, bell peppers, and scallion in the bowl of a food processor and purée until smooth. Cover and refrigerate for 2 to 4 hours.

Pour a film of oil into a 7- or 8-inch sauté pan over medium heat. Ladle in about 2 tablespoons of batter, and cook it until it's slightly browned. Flip the crêpe and continue cooking for another minute until it's cooked through. Transfer to a plate and repeat to cook the remaining crêpes, stacking them on top of one another. You should have 4 to 6 crêpes.

Preheat the oven to 400°F.

Wrap 2 or 3 tablespoons of duck confit with a tablespoon of sauce in each corn crêpe to make a cylinder. Arrange the crêpes, seam side down, in a baking dish. Bake until heated through, about 10 minutes. Divide among four plates and garnish with a little sour cream.

The Power of the Pierogi

Once word of mouth began to spread about the food we were doing, more and more people were asking us exactly what kind of food we served. Liz said, "Michael, what should I tell them?"

I didn't know. "American?" I suggested.

"What's that?"

"I don't know, Liz, it's influenced by all kinds of things. I'm just doing the food I like. What is it? It's Midwestern food. Tell people it's Midwestern cuisine."

Liz stopped and stared at me. "What are you f—ing crazy? We'll be out of business in a week! What the hell does that mean?"

She's always been more sensible than me, but we stuck with Midwestern anyway and today refer to it as heritage Midwestern.

There's no real consensus on what Midwestern cuisine is. I am happy to say that—due to recent interest in local ingredients and the great ones we have here, from mushrooms to fish to berries—Midwestern food no longer carries such a stigma. The Midwest is a mix of Eastern and Northern European, Russian, Mediterranean, African, and Indian immigrants.

Cleveland is a melting pot. And I have always cooked to the Cleveland I knew, and what I loved, which is food that has a lot of Mediterranean influences, but also Eastern European influences. I still think of Lola as being more closely related to Eastern Europe on my dad's and my granddad's side, and its younger sister restaurant, Lolita, as being more closely linked to my Greek and Italian mom.

The question for me was how to cook the food I cared about and get my conservative city to accept it and like it. Almost always I did this by sort of meeting them halfway. When I got to the Caxton after Giovanni's in 1994, every restaurant in town had fried calamari on the menu, and people who came to the Caxton expected to see it. But every restaurant in town did the same old calamari and marinara sauce. I love ginger and thought that would be a cool way to flavor the calamari. I ended up soaking it in ginger ale and tossing it in flour mixed with dried and pulverized gingerroot, and served it with a green onion aioli. It was delicious, it made my customers happy, and it made me happy.

The key to success, I eventually learned, is to present new or unfamiliar ingredients in a familiar setting, so that people aren't intimidated.

Enter the humble pierogi. If there is one preparation most representative of the city of Cleveland, it's the pierogi, a big boiled dumpling filled, traditionally, with potatoes and cheese. It's a staple of Eastern Europe, common in the cuisines of Russia, Ukraine, Poland, Latvia, and Slovakia—ethnicities that are pervasive in Cleveland. And so are pierogies; people are very familiar with them. They're comfort food.

Beef cheeks, however, were not initially comforting to Clevelanders in the 1990s. The idea of eating any cheek meet was foreign to them and therefore to be avoided. While this heavily worked muscle results in a deeply satisfying braise, I'd never have been able to serve a straightforward dish of braised beef cheeks, the way I could serve a braised lamb shank or osso bucco. Ah, but if I slipped some of this succulent tender braised beef cheek inside some of my grandfather's pierogi dough, boiled them, then fried them crispy on the outside and served them topped with some mushrooms and a creamy horseradish sauce, people were willing to try it. Now it's Lola's most popular dish, one that symbolizes what Lola is: we took the intimidation out of fine dining and helped people to eat outside the box even though they didn't realize they were doing just that.

My menus are filled with this kind of twist on common American culinary idioms. Tater tots became crab tater tots to accompany grouper. Mac and cheese evolved as a pasta dish with rosemary and goat cheese. People in this town love their brats, and I love to serve foie gras, so I put foie gras in the form of a brat on the menu and people embraced it.

This is what I mean by approachable food: food that doesn't intimidate, but also that doesn't compromise at all; food that's fun to eat, that makes you happy.

BEEF CHEEK PIEROGIES WITH WILD MUSHROOMS AND HORSERADISH

If have a signature dish, it's this, a sour-cream-enriched dough from Pap, my dad's dad, filled with beef cheek that's been braised until it's meltingly tender. Traditionally the dough is filled with potatoes and cheese and boiled, then served with some sauerkraut or some caramelized onions on top. But I wanted to make my pierogies a little more special.

These can be made a day or two in advance through the braising stage and then covered and refrigerated. The pierogies can be made and refrigerated for up to four days before cooking them, or frozen for up to three months. Finish them quickly at the last minute for an excellent, and special, dish for entertaining. The recipe may look daunting, and there are a few steps, but none of them is particularly difficult.

This recipe makes enough filling for about thirty 3-inch pierogies. You may have leftover filling; it's delicious with pasta, on a toasted baguette, or inside a Corn Crêpe (see page 40).

Like the corn crêpe, the pierogi is a vehicle for other flavors and garnishes:

- If you can't find beef cheeks, cubed beef shoulder or pork shoulder can be substituted.
- Any leftover braised meat you might have—such as from beef stew, pulled pork, or osso bucco—would make a great filling, as would duck confit.
- You can always go classic with mashed potatoes and cheese filling. Other vegetarian versions can be made using sautéed spinach or seared mushrooms.
- Finally, I've even made dessert pierogies, filled with bananas sautéed with brown sugar, and topped with caramel sauce and hazelnuts. In a sweet European version, they're stuffed with stewed prunes.

To me nothing screams Cleveland more than the humble pierogi.

Serves 8 to 10

Pierogi Dough

1 large egg
¾ cup sour cream
8 tablespoons (1 stick) unsalted butter, softened

1 tablespoon chopped fresh chives
1 teaspoon kosher salt
2 cups all-purpose flour, plus more for rolling dough

recipe continued on next page

Beef Cheeks

2 tablespoons olive oil
1½ pounds cleaned beef cheeks
Kosher salt and freshly ground black
  pepper
1 cup all-purpose flour
1 red onion, sliced
1 carrot, peeled and sliced
2 garlic cloves, smashed with the flat side
  of a knife

¼ cup red wine vinegar
1 cup red wine
4 sprigs of fresh thyme
1 bay leaf
2 cups Chicken Stock (page 131)
4 tablespoons (½ stick) unsalted butter
Seared Wild Mushrooms (page 158)
Horseradish Crème Frâiche (page 139)

To make the dough, work the egg, sour cream, butter, chives, and salt together by hand to form a dough. Don't worry if the mixture is not uniform and, as with pie dough, don't overwork it. Pour the flour onto a work surface and make a well in the center. Add the sour cream mixture and mix thoroughly with your hands until a dough forms. Wrap in plastic and refrigerate the dough for at least 2 hours or up to 2 days.

To braise the beef cheeks, preheat the oven to 325°F.

Heat the olive oil in a large enameled cast-iron Dutch oven over medium-high heat. Season the cheeks with salt and pepper, and then dredge them in flour, shaking off excess. Cook them in batches, turning as needed, until browned, about 6 minutes. Transfer the cheeks to a plate.

Add the onion and carrot to the Dutch oven and cook over moderate heat until softened, seasoning with salt as you do, about 7 minutes. Add the garlic and cook a minute longer. Add the vinegar, red wine, thyme, bay leaf, and chicken stock and bring to a simmer. Return the beef cheeks to the Dutch oven, then cover, and braise in the oven for 1 hour.

Lower the oven temperature to 225°F. and cook for 4 hours, or until the meat is very tender. Remove from the oven, allow to cool, and then chill in the refrigerator in the cooking liquid for at least 4 hours or up to 2 days.

Remove the chilled cheeks from the liquid and shred the meat. Set aside the meat.

Strain the liquid into a saucepan and boil over high heat to reduce by two thirds. Remove from the heat and let cool until the liquid becomes gelatinous. Return the meat to the liquid and stir together.

Roll out the dough on a lightly floured work surface to a ⅛-inch thickness and cut it into 3-inch rounds. Spoon 1 tablespoon of meat onto each round. Fold the dough over into half-moons and press the edges with a fork to seal them.

Bring 2 gallons of salted water to a rolling boil. Add the pierogies and wait until they float. Cook for 4 minutes, starting the timing once the pierogies float. Drain well in a colander.

To serve, heat the butter in a large skillet until it froths. Add the pierogies and cook until golden brown and hot all the way through, about 2 minutes per side. You may need to work in batches depending on the size of your pan, keeping cooked pierogies in a hot oven until ready to serve.

Serve with the seared wild mushrooms and the horseradish crème frâiche.

Soups and Sandwiches

Soup is a category of cooking that is so wonderful because it can be, must be, thought of seasonally. We eat roasted or grilled meats all year round, sautéed or poached fish in every season, but you'd never serve a fresh corn soup in the dead of winter or a hearty hot bean soup at the height of summer. You're going to serve a corn soup when corn is abundant and delicious, in the summer. And in the fall or winter you're going to want to make a rich chicken and dumpling soup. Soup is determined by the season.

Another thing I love about soup is that there are no rules: from vegetables to starches, meats, and fish, there's nothing that doesn't go well in a soup. I could look in your fridge at pretty much any time and find six ingredients that go together in a liquid to make a delicious soup. Soup gives you great flexibility as a cook.

I think stock is important—it gives a soup a base, a depth that you can't get with canned broth or water—but the great thing about most soups is that you can create the stock as you're making the soup. Meat and vegetables are what make stock, and they make soup, too. You can put a chicken in a pot with some vegetables and cover it with water, and if you give it enough cooking time, it will give you that depth of flavor you need in a soup. The same strategy can be used with tomato sauce (see page 229); this requires a long cooking time, so if you don't have homemade beef stock to fortify it, you can put some beef or veal or even chicken bones in there to give the sauce great depth. Tomatoes also can be used to circumvent stock altogether; they will give you an excellent soup base, as will vegetable purées, which can achieve great body and flavor.

Sandwiches, on the other hand, are great anytime, all the time, year-round, for breakfast, lunch, or dinner; the only thing that limits your sandwich repertoire is your imagination.

I compose a sandwich the way I do a finished dish on a plate: it should achieve a balance of textures and flavors. Just as soups need a great base, so, too, do sandwiches. And that base is bread, of course. You need a great bread—hard or soft, depending on the sandwich, but I usually prefer a sturdy bread. A sandwich always needs some crunch, if you ask me. Potato chips are one of my favorite ingredients to put on sandwiches, but you can also get crunch from raw vegetables or lettuces. Sandwiches need a creamy element, like mayonnaise, aioli, or cheese. And of course they need a little bit of acid, whether from something like a tomato or a smear of mustard, or—you guessed it—pickled vegetables. Add a little bit of heat if you wish, some chilies, fresh or pickled.

The only sandwich that doesn't fit any rules is peanut butter, honey, and banana—which Liz makes for me—toasted in a pan. I guess you could say it's a sandwich that can be eaten for breakfast, lunch, dinner, or dessert!

Sweating and Caramelizing

Two techniques that I use a lot, and that are very important to flavoring a dish—everything from soups and sauces to braises—are sweating and caramelizing.

Sweating an onion or any aromatic vegetable means cooking it gently in a little oil or butter until it becomes translucent without giving it any color or browning it in any way (which would create sweeter, more complex flavors). Try to keep the ingredient in a single layer so that it cooks evenly. Sweating will deepen the aromatic's effect on the finished dish and is very important. Generally, the longer you sweat vegetables, the greater the final flavor impact.

I always hit the vegetables with a little salt as they're sweating, which helps to extract moisture, concentrating flavor, and begins the seasoning process for the finished dish. I never miss an opportunity to sweat.

In addition to vegetables, fish bones and the shells from shellfish to be used for stock are usually sweated as well, again to develop flavor.

Caramelizing, which means cooking vegetables until they brown, adds a different and complex sweetness to the finished dish. Part of the browning comes from actual caramelization of the natural sugars in the vegetable, but there is other browning going on in the process as well. Whereas sweating is always done in the service of some other dish, sometimes caramelization is an end in itself: caramelized onions are a great topping for steak and are the main ingredient in onion soup, for example; and I might caramelize endive to use as a side dish.

Both sweating and caramelizing are done over low heat, though caramelization requires a little higher heat. When you're sweating vegetables, if the heat is too high, they'll brown. The browning of sugars and carbohydrates happens at temperatures well above boiling, so browning can't occur in a moist environment. You need to cook off much of a vegetable's moisture before it will begin to brown. But you have to do this slowly; if you try to do it quickly by using high heat, you might burn the food instead, making the vegetable bitter rather than intensely sweet.

Generally, for lighter stock and sauces, the aromatics should be sweated. For brown sauces and for darker, sweeter, more complex preparations such as braises, the aromatics can be caramelized.

Sweating and caramelizing aromatic vegetables are used not just in these soups but throughout all the cooking I do. I rarely put a raw vegetable into a stock or a sauce. The more attention you give to these techniques, the better your finished dish will be.

SWEET CORN AND WILD MUSHROOM SOUP

This soup is for summer, when corn is at its peak. It uses a simple, great technique: it makes a stock from the corn cobs. How many corn cobs have people thrown out, not realizing how much flavor is still in them? When you simmer the cobs—after you've cut off the kernels—all the remaining milk from the corn is released into the water, creating a really flavorful broth. You can make all kinds of soups with it and you can also use it to make sauces; try this corn cob stock in a hot vinaigrette (see page 187) and serve it with seafood, for instance.

Instead of making a roux I purée half the corn in a Vitamix blender and return it to the soup to give it a luxurious texture. (If you don't have a Vitamix you can use a regular blender and give the liquid a quick strain if it isn't smooth.) And I garnish it with flavors that taste fantastic with corn: mushrooms and bacon.

Serves 6 to 8

Corn Cob Stock

6 ears of corn
1 red onion, chopped
2 garlic cloves, sliced
2 sprigs of fresh thyme

1 tablespoon coriander seeds, toasted
   (see Symon Says, page 69)
2 quarts (8 cups) Chicken Stock
   (page 131) or water
1 teaspoon kosher salt

Soup

2 tablespoons corn oil
1 garlic clove, minced
1 teaspoon fresh thyme leaves

1 cup heavy cream
1 cup Seared Wild Mushrooms (page 158)
½ cup crumbled cooked bacon

To make the corn cob stock, cut the kernels from the cobs and reserve the kernels for the soup. Toss the cobs into a large pot with the onion, garlic, rosemary, coriander, stock, and salt. Bring to a boil, lower the heat, and simmer for 45 minutes. Strain the liquid through a fine-mesh strainer, discarding the solids. You should have about 4 cups. The stock will keep in the refrigerator overnight.

To make the soup, heat the oil in a 4-quart pan over medium heat. Add the garlic and sweat it for 2 minutes. Add the reserved corn kernels and continue to sweat the mixture, stirring with a wooden spoon, for 3 minutes. Add the thyme, corn stock, and cream and simmer for 45 minutes.

Remove about half the corn with a slotted spoon and purée it in a blender with enough of the liquid to get it moving. Whisk the puréed corn back into the soup and return the soup to a simmer. Divide the soup among six to eight bowls and garnish with the mushrooms and bacon.

CHICKEN AND DUMPLING SOUP

Pap, my granddad, made this soup for just about every holiday I can remember, and for me it remains bound up with family and celebration and love. It would be years later that I learned that the dumpling dough had a fancy name, *pâte à choux,* which is an excellent and versatile dough, but here, it's just a dumpling, enriched with chicken fat (rather than the traditional butter) and seasoned with fresh tarragon. At the restaurant, we serve these with walleye, but even for that dish we cut the dumpling dough straight off the board and into the pot. This recipe can be done all at once, but it's best to start this a day before you want to serve in order to de-fat the stock (and use the fat for the dumplings!).

Serves 6 to 8

Soup

1 tablespoon unsalted butter
2 carrots, finely diced
2 parsnips, finely diced
1 onion, finely diced
1 celery root, finely diced
4 garlic cloves, minced

Kosher salt
2 quarts (8 cups) Chicken Stock (page 131) or water
1 3-pound chicken, preferably organic or naturally raised
2 bay leaves

Dumplings

Unsalted butter, if needed
1 cup whole milk
½ teaspoon kosher salt
½ teaspoon freshly ground black pepper

½ teaspoon grated nutmeg
1 cup all-purpose flour
2 teaspoons chopped fresh tarragon
3 large eggs

To make the soup, melt the butter in a large soup pot over medium heat. Add the carrots, parsnips, onion, celery root, garlic, and a good three-finger pinch of salt. Sweat the vegetables, stirring occasionally, for 2 to 3 minutes. Add the stock and bring it to a simmer. Season with salt to taste and then add the chicken and bay leaves. Bring the stock back up to a simmer, skimming all the foam and congealing protein that the chicken releases. Reduce the heat to medium low and simmer for 1 hour, or until the chicken is cooked through.

Remove the chicken from the pot and allow to cool enough to handle comfortably. Pick all the meat from it, shredding it by hand and discarding the skin and bones. Discard the bay leaves. Cover and refrigerate the meat and soup separately overnight or until the soup is thoroughly chilled.

Remove the fat that has congealed on top of the soup and reserve it for the dumplings. Set the soup over medium-low heat and allow it to come gradually back up to a simmer while you make the dumplings.

To make the dumplings, measure the reserved chicken fat. You need ½ cup. If necessary, add butter to make ½ cup. In a medium saucepan over medium-high heat, bring the milk and fat to a simmer. Add the salt, pepper, and nutmeg. Remove the pan from the heat and add the flour, stirring with a heavy wooden spoon until the flour has absorbed all the milk and the resulting dough pulls away from the sides of the pan. Add the tarragon and then the eggs, one at a time, stirring until each egg is incorporated.

Drop, scoop, or cut the dough one tablespoon at a time into the soup. My method is to wet a cutting board and press portions of the sticky dough into thin sheets about ¼ inch thick and 1½ inches wide, then cut into about ½-inch pieces, and scrape them into the soup. Simmer the dough for about 10 minutes, then add the chicken, returning to a simmer, and serve.

SPICY TOMATO AND BLUE CHEESE SOUP

There's always an exception to every rule, and my tomato soup is it. It's one soup that can be made all year round because canned San Marzanos are consistently good. This is a dish, God, I've been making it since my time at Players nearly twenty years ago. It's so easy and so delicious that it was my long-time chef Frankie Rogers's go-to soup, the get-myself-out-of-the-weeds soup. San Marzano tomatoes, some aromatic vegetables, sriracha sauce (one of my favorite condiments, available in most supermarkets in the ethic aisle and in Asian markets) for heat, and blue cheese for richness. It comes together in no time.

Serves 4 to 6

2 tablespoons olive oil
1 medium red onion, finely chopped
Kosher salt
4 garlic cloves, sliced
1 28-ounce can San Marzano tomatoes,
 with their juice

1½ cups Chicken Stock (page 131)
¾ cup heavy cream
2 tablespoons sriracha sauce
1 tablespoon fresh oregano leaves
½ cup Roth Käse Buttermilk Blue cheese
 (see Sources, page 250)

Heat the olive oil in a 4-quart pot over medium heat. When the oil is hot, add the onion and a three-fingered pinch of salt and sweat for 2 minutes. Add the garlic and continue to sweat for 2 more minutes. Add the tomatoes, their juice, and the stock and bring to a simmer. Add the cream, sriracha sauce, and oregano and simmer for 45 minutes.

 Pour the soup into a blender, add the blue cheese, and blend until smooth, working in batches if needed. Strain through a fine-mesh strainer into a clean pot, taste, adjust the seasoning if necessary, and reheat to serve. The soup will keep, covered in the refrigerator, for a few days.

BBLT (BELLY, BACON, LETTUCE, AND TOMATO)

This is my pork love child. It combines two forms of pork belly: braised pork belly that you sauté until crisp and serve warm and cured, and smoked pork belly, aka bacon. With all this great fat, you need some serious contrast, and it's provided by spicy chile, peppery greens, and acidic pickled tomato.

Serves 1

1 6-inch piece of Braised Pork Belly
   (page 216), sliced ⅓ inch thick
1 6-inch French roll
1 tablespoon Aioli (page 141)
2 slices crisp cooked bacon

1 pickled chile (see page 120), thinly
   sliced
1 pickled green tomato (see page 122),
   sliced
¼ cup loosely packed fresh watercress

Heat a medium sauté pan over high heat. When the pan is hot, brown the pork belly slices until they're crisp, about 2 minutes per side. Split the roll, slather with the aioli, and layer the pork belly, bacon, chili, tomato, and watercress inside. Serve.

SOPPRESSATA SANDWICH WITH FRIED EGG AND SHASHA SAUCE

When I was growing up, my dad was the king of the sandwich. He unfailingly came up with different concoctions for my sister Nikki and me. Some were good, some horrendous—never try bologna and peanut butter!! But it turned me into a sandwich junkie. The egg here plays along really well with the spicy soppressata, an Italian dry-cured sausage, and makes this a great sandwich for breakfast, lunch, or a light dinner. Frying the generously larded soppressata crisps up the meat and gives the sandwich body. But it's also efficient, because you use that same pan to make a sunny-side-up egg, glazing it with the spicy rendered fat. (You can also use the fat to cook onions, peppers, or greens for a flavor boost with no extra work.) This sandwich has great balance: the saltiness of the meat is offset by the sweetness of the basil and the creaminess of the egg and mozzarella.

My mother-in-law Sherla's "Shasha" sauce, with its mustard and vinegar flavors and light sweetness, is the perfect foil to complete this sandwich. Any bread will work, but I really love this with some grilled sourdough. Double, triple, or quadruple this recipe at will.

Serves 1

2 paper-thin slices red onion

4 to 6 thin slices (about 4 ounces) soppressata or dry-cured Italian salami

1 large egg

2 slices (about 2 ounces) prosciutto

2 thin slices (about 2 ounces) fresh mozzarella

2 thick slices sourdough bread, toasted or grilled

4 large fresh basil leaves

2 tablespoons Shasha Sauce (page 138)

Soak the onion in a small bowl of ice water for 2 minutes.

While the onion is soaking, in a medium nonstick sauté pan over low heat, fry the soppressata over medium-high heat until lightly crisp and some fat has rendered, about 2 minutes per side. Remove it to a plate. In the same pan, fry an egg sunny-side up.

While the egg is cooking, drain the onion slices and layer the soppressata, prosciutto, mozzarella, and onion slices on a slice of bread. Top with the other slice and place the sandwich in the pan next to the egg, pressing down on the sandwich with the palm of your hand. When that side is lightly toasted, about 3 or 4 minutes, flip the sandwich and toast the other side.

Remove the sandwich to a cutting board, and open the sandwich. Lay down the basil leaves, place the egg in the center, and spoon on the Shasha sauce. Close the sandwich and slice it in half to serve.

SYMON SAYS

Soaking sliced onion in ice water is something I learned from my mom. It takes the raw bite out of the onion and keeps it light and crunchy.

There are very few sandwiches that aren't improved when you put a fried egg on top.

THE LOLA BURGER

I'm sorry—I'm gonna say it: this is the best hamburger ever. A great burger is all about the meat. Make sure you don't buy super-lean ground beef or your burger will be dry and flavorless. Better still, grind your own meat. I recommend you use equal parts brisket, beef cheek, and sirloin, the cuts I use at Lola, and they'll yield about a 75 to 25 meat-to-fat ratio, which is what you want for a great burger. But even more important than the cut of meat, is the grind. The best texture results from passing your meat through the large die (¼ inch), twice. This is more important than the actual cut, provided you retain the three parts meat and one part fat ratio.

We also have some great toppings to set this burger apart. Instead of hamburger buns, we put these on English muffins—Bays English muffins, to be exact, which are the most flavorful. Shape the burgers slightly larger than your muffins to make up for shrinkage. We also serve bacon and a fried egg on these. Cook your bacon ahead of time and you can fry your eggs in the bacon fat as soon as you take the burgers off the grill, while they're resting.

Serves 4

8 slices bacon
24 ounces ground beef, 75 percent lean
 (see headnote)
Kosher salt and cracked black pepper
4 thin slices cheddar cheese

4 English muffins, split
4 large eggs
1 dill pickle, thinly sliced
½ cup pickled red onion (see page 117)
4 teaspoons Spicy Ketchup (page 133)

Build a medium-hot fire in your grill or preheat a stovetop grill pan.

Cook the bacon in a sauté pan over medium-high heat, turning once, until crisp, 5 minutes. Remove the bacon to paper towels to drain. Reserve the bacon fat in the pan.

Form the ground beef into 4 patties, each about 3½ inches in diameter. Season the patties liberally with kosher salt and cracked black pepper. Place the burgers on the grill or in the grill pan and cook for 3 minutes. Flip and top each burger with a slice of cheese. Grill for 3 minutes for medium rare. Remove to a plate. Add the English muffins to the grill or grill pan and toast for 1 minute.

Cook the eggs sunny-side up in the bacon fat while the burgers rest.

Build the burgers by sandwiching them between the muffin halves along with pickle slices, red onion, bacon, an egg, and some spicy ketchup.

Salads

Most people tend to think of salads as lettuce with dressing, but they're so much more than that. Salad to me is a composed plate like any other and it needs to hit all my benchmarks for a great dish. It often has meat or fish or egg, roasted vegetables, freshly sliced fruits, and greens. I like to serve them warm and cold, and the choice of vinaigrette brings everything together. A simple salad of lettuce with dressing is better after the meal, European style. The following are examples of hearty salads, big bright vivid plates that I like to serve as a first or main course—shaved fennel and orange, for example; spinach, mushroom, and egg; or roasted beets with blue cheese.

Vinaigrettes

Vinaigrettes are a powerful tool for building flavors. I love their versatility in that they can be used to dress a salad, as can all of the recipes here, but they can also be used to finish a sauce (see The Power of the Hot Vinaigrette on page 187) or to cut through some of the richness of meats; Fresh Bacon with Watermelon and Haloumi (page 219) is sauced with a vinaigrette, for example.

They're so easy, made from such humble and readily available ingredients, that it always amazes me that more people don't make them at home. They can be put together in seconds and are a lot cheaper to make yourself than to buy—plus you know everything that is going into them and don't have to worry about the additives that go into most processed salad dressings.

The other great thing about making vinaigrettes yourself is that you can control the acidity levels to your taste. The traditional ratio for a vinaigrette is three parts oil to one part vinegar. But I tend to like things a little bit on the bitey side so the ratios that I give are a little more tart. The best way to achieve the right level of acidity for you is simply to taste the vinaigrette as you're adding the oil and stop or add more to please your palate. Remember as you're tasting, though, that you're not going to be eating your vinaigrette plain, so err at first on the side of too much acidity and then scale up your use of oil accordingly.

I start all my vinaigrettes with some minced shallot and garlic, which are first combined with the acid, whether that's lemon juice or vinegar. The acidic component immediately neutralizes the sharpness of raw garlic and shallot, and magnifies their aromatic and sweet effects. I build the vinaigrette from this base. The basic technique is always the same: Combine the acid, garlic, shallot, and salt (so that the salt melts; it's harder to incorporate salt once the fat has been added), and then slowly whisk in the oil. If you want to add additional fresh herbs, do so just before serving the vinaigrette. A basic vinaigrette, without aromatics, will keep for a week refrigerated. Once aromatics have been added to a vinaigrette, it will keep only for about a day.

RED WINE VINAIGRETTE

The red wine vinaigrette is the workhorse and goes with just about everything—salads, braised meats, tomatoes, and vegetables. The exception is fish, which work better with a citrus vinaigrette.

Makes about 1½ cups

1 tablespoon minced shallot
1 teaspoon minced garlic
½ cup red wine vinegar
½ teaspoon kosher salt
1¼ cups extra-virgin olive oil

1 tablespoon chopped toasted almonds
    (optional; to toast nuts, see page 69)
1 teaspoon diced seeded fresno chile
    pepper (optional)
2 tablespoons sliced fresh mint (optional)

Combine the shallot, garlic, vinegar, and salt in a medium mixing bowl. Whisk in a few drops of the oil and then begin adding the oil in a thin stream, whisking continuously. After all the oil has been incorporated, whisk in any optional ingredients you may be using.

BALSAMIC VINAIGRETTE

This is a slightly sweeter vinaigrette that is good for salads and drizzled over tomatoes and grilled meats.

Makes about 1½ cups

1 tablespoon minced shallot
1 teaspoon minced garlic
½ cup balsamic vinegar
1 tablespoon Dijon mustard

1 tablespoon honey
¼ teaspoon kosher salt
1 cup extra-virgin olive oil

Combine the shallot, garlic, balsamic vinegar, mustard, honey, and salt in a medium mixing bowl. Whisk in a few drops of the oil and then begin adding the oil in a thin stream, whisking continuously until all the oil is incorporated.

SHERRY VINAIGRETTE

Use this vinaigrette for salads, seafood, poultry, and vegetables. A good Spanish sherry vinegar is worth the extra expense, especially when its flavor is front and center, as in a vinaigrette.

Makes about 1 ¾ cups

1 tablespoon minced shallot
1 tablespoon minced garlic
½ cup sherry vinegar

1 teaspoon Dijon mustard
¼ teaspoon kosher salt
1 cup extra-virgin olive oil

Combine the shallot, garlic, vinegar, mustard, and salt in a medium mixing bowl. Whisk in a few drops of the oil and then begin adding the oil in a thin stream, whisking continuously until all the oil is incorporated.

ORANGE VINAIGRETTE

Try this aromatic vinaigrette with seafood, poultry, salads, and roasted vegetables. This is a particularly great vinaigrette for beet salads.

Makes about 1¼ cups

1 cup freshly squeezed orange juice
1 tablespoon minced shallot
1 teaspoon minced garlic
1 teaspoon finely chopped fresh
   rosemary

¼ teaspoon cracked black pepper
¼ teaspoon kosher salt
¾ cup extra-virgin olive oil

In a small nonreactive saucepan, bring the orange juice to a simmer. Cook until reduced by half, about 5 minutes. Transfer to a bowl and cool to room temperature.

  Combine the juice with the shallot, garlic, rosemary, pepper, and salt in a medium mixing bowl. Whisk in a few drops of the oil and then begin adding the oil in a thin stream, whisking continuously until all the oil is incorporated.

LEMON VINAIGRETTE

This brightly flavored vinaigrette is excellent with fish, shellfish, and poultry, as well as crisp lettuces such as romaine.

Makes about 1½ cups

1 tablespoon minced shallot
1 teaspoon minced garlic
½ cup fresh lemon juice

¼ teaspoon kosher salt
¾ cup extra-virgin olive oil
1 tablespoon chopped fresh dill (optional)

Combine the shallot, garlic, lemon juice, and salt in a medium mixing bowl. Whisk in a few drops of the oil and then begin adding the oil in a thin stream, whisking continuously until all the oil is incorporated. Add the dill, if using, right before serving.

Seasoning Beyond Salt: Herbs, Spices, and Aromatics

When I ask one of my chefs de cuisine, Derek Clayton or Matthew Harlan—aka Powder and Chatty, respectively—to put together a new dish, they will normally phrase their first question this way: "OK, so besides garlic, shallot, lemon, and coriander, what do you want in it?"

It almost doesn't matter what the dish is. If French cuisine gives us an onion-carrot-celery mirepoix and New Orleans gives us a Cajun mirepoix of garlic, onion, and bell pepper, then my mirepoix is garlic-shallot-lemon-coriander.

This combination forms the backbone of my cooking. The ingredients appear in various proportions to one another, depending on the dish, and they don't always go together, but I've found that more dishes than not benefit from some combination of this powerful quartet. Cinnamon almost belongs in this group as well; it's very strong, is not as versatile as any in the quartet, and needs to be used judiciously, but I use it frequently in savory dishes.

Knowing how to buy and use spices is important. There are a few simple rules: buy them whole whenever possible, buy them in small quantities to ensure that they're always fresh, and toast them before you crush or grind them. Toasting your coriander and cumin, or any whole seeds or berries, releases the oils that make them such powerful seasoning devices.

My number-one favorite spice: Coriander

There is no more balanced spice in your pantry than coriander. This seed of the coriander, or cilantro, plant is unique in another way: besides being balanced, it works with almost every food, and it's almost impossible to overseason food with it. You can give meats a thick crust of cracked coriander seeds, or give a sauce a teaspoon of pulverized coriander seeds, and its effects are equally powerful. Think about other spices: peppercorns, cumin, chilies, allspice, nutmeg, cinnamon—every one of them can be overused, can overpower a dish. From a standpoint of both flavor and aroma, coriander is both subtle and powerful. I love the citrusy notes it brings to food, similar to the flavor of burnt orange. Coarsely cracked, it's beautiful on grilled lamb chops, adding aroma, flavor, and crunch. Powdered, it's wonderful in sauces. I use it almost across the board; coriander is my ally in the kitchen.

Cinnamon

Cinnamon is a powerful spice in savory dishes. I love it in shellfish sauces, and it adds subtle depth to the braising liquid for lamb and veal shank and to tomato sauces. But it's very, very tricky to get right and can ruin those dishes, too. What I recommend, to give you more control when you're seasoning sauces, is to use cinnamon sticks and taste the sauces as they're cooking. When the cinnamon flavor hits the right pitch, remove the cinnamon stick. You can't do this if you use powdered cinnamon.

Herbs

I love all fresh herbs, and I rarely if ever use dried herbs because I can't know their quality and what level of intensity they will bring to a dish.

Herbs are divided into two categories, hard and soft. Hard herbs are the ones that have thick, woody stems: oregano, sage, thyme, lavender, and rosemary, for example. These are typically powerful herbs that are added at the beginning of a dish and can withstand the heat, slowly releasing their oils and flavors. Because they're so strong, they can easily overwhelm a dish.

Soft herbs include basil, dill, cilantro, tarragon, parsley, chives, and chervil. They are more delicate and volatile. These herbs should only be used at the end of cooking, after the pan is off the heat and you're ready to serve the dish. My mom will spend a lot of money on basil, then throw it into a sauce she's gonna cook for seven hours—drives me crazy. Don't cut your soft herbs too much. Mincing them will destroy their flavor. The only herb I cut fine is chives. As a rule, give soft herbs one pass with the knife just before you use them, or better, tear the leaves by hand.

SYMON SAYS

To toast whole spices (or nuts), simply pour them—one variety at a time, since different spices toast at different speeds—in a dry sauté pan and toast, tossing occasionally, over medium heat until fragrant, 2 to 3 minutes. Transfer them to a plate to cool. To grind the spices, put them in a spice mill, coffee grinder, or mortar and pestle, and grind just before you add them to your dish. You can also simply give them a rough chop on your cutting board.

Herb Credo: If I Had To Choose

Among the hard herbs, the herb that works well with just about anything is thyme. But for impact, nothing beats rosemary, my favorite hard herb. Yes, it can overpower, so you have to be careful using it. And I think it usually overpowers seafood. But it's great with most meats and is especially good with starchy vegetables. On French fries, it's the best.

Parsley is the workhorse of the soft herbs because it has so many uses, from seasoning and finishing dishes to being used as an aromatic in sauces and soups. Mint is up there for me; I use a lot of that as well. But my favorite soft herb is dill. While it simply doesn't go with any red meat, it's delicious with seafood, salads, and white meats. I love it with potatoes, with roasted beets, with tomatoes. Everybody wants to put basil with tomatoes, but I like dill better. To me dill has a magical flavor, especially when combined with lemon, garlic, and shallots.

Shallot and Garlic

These great aromatics are invaluable, adding sweetness and depth in almost all savory preparations. But they're not one-note players. You can manipulate them in the way you cook them. Cook them gently and they become sweet. Cook them more aggressively and more caramel notes begin to come out. With garlic, when it's browned, it becomes nutty and has a great flavor on its own. Caramelized shallots are a hugely influential seasoning in sauces and vinaigrettes. It's important that you buy them whole; don't buy peeled garlic and shallots, and certainly never buy prechopped. Those products have lost all their sweetness and have become somewhat bitter from the heat of the processing machines.

Lemon

Lemon brings great acidity to a dish, but it's a balanced acidity, in terms of both flavor and sweetness. Again, like coriander, it's this balance that makes it so useful. We don't usually think of the sweetness of lemons, but they do have a sweetness. On the citrus continuum, oranges have high sweetness and a lower acidity. Limes have great acidity relative to their sweetness. And lemons fall somewhere in between.

SPINACH SALAD WITH FRIED EGG, BACON, AND MORELS

In Ohio in the 1970s a party wasn't a party unless you served a warm spinach salad topped with bacon bits, button mushrooms, hard-boiled egg, and a dressing made with ketchup. I'd lay odds it was someone's attempt to recreate a traditional frisée and lardons salad using what was available in the Midwest at the time. I've taken this mainstay from my childhood uptown with our house-smoked bacon, morel mushrooms, and an egg, dressed with a balsamic vinaigrette (hold the ketchup). I love eggs on salad; poached eggs on a spinach salad are traditional, but I prefer fried. If you don't make your own bacon (page 98), I recommend Nueske's from Wisconsin (see Sources, page 250).

Serves 4

2 teaspoons extra-virgin olive oil,
   or more as needed
8 ounces slab bacon, cut into 1-inch by
   ¼-inch pieces
1 shallot, thinly sliced
6 ounces morel mushrooms,
   halved if large
½ cup Chicken Stock (page 131) or water

6 tablespoons balsamic vinegar,
   or more to taste
4 large eggs
Kosher salt and freshly ground black
   pepper
8 ounces fresh spinach leaves (about
   8 cups loosely packed), stemmed

Heat a sauté pan glazed with 1 teaspoon of the olive oil over medium-high heat. Add the bacon pieces and sauté them until they develop a crispy exterior but remain tender on the inside, adjusting the heat as necessary, 5 to 10 minutes. Add the shallot and sauté until it is translucent, another minute or two. Add the mushrooms, and once they begin to soften, after about 2 minutes, add the stock, scraping the browned bits from the bottom of the pan as the liquid comes to a boil. Reduce the pan liquid by half. Add the balsamic vinegar, bring to a simmer, and then remove the pan from the heat. Taste the pan sauce looking for a proper balance of fat and acidity. If the sauce tastes too fatty, add another dash of balsamic. If it's too acidic, correct it with additional extra-virgin olive oil.

Heat a large nonstick pan over medium-low heat. Glaze the pan with the remaining teaspoon of olive oil and crack in the eggs, taking care not to break the yolks. Season each egg with a pinch of salt and some black pepper. Fry the eggs gently until the whites are cooked through but the yolks remain runny.

Place the spinach in a large bowl. Pour the warm dressing, with the bacon and morels, over the spinach and toss until the leaves are wilted and coated.

Divide the spinach salad among four plates and top each with a fried egg.

SHAVED FENNEL SALAD WITH ORANGES, LEMON, DILL, AND WATERCRESS

Fennel may be my favorite vegetable because it's so versatile: you can eat it raw, you can shave it, you can roast it, braise it, pickle it, stuff it into birds, sauté it, garnish with it, use it as an aromatic, make it into a main course or side dish. How many vegetables can you do that with?

This is a refreshing salad of raw, shaved fennel with orange and dill. It works well as a side salad or it can be used as a base for a lean white fish.

Serves 4

3 oranges
1 garlic clove, minced
1 shallot, thinly sliced, soaked in cold water for 10 minutes and drained
¼ teaspoon kosher salt
Grated zest and juice of 1 lemon
2 small or 1 large fennel bulb, core removed, shaved

1 tablespoon coarsely chopped fennel fronds
2 tablespoons coarsely chopped fresh dill
Freshly ground black pepper
¼ teaspoon ground coriander
2 tablespoons extra-virgin olive oil
1 cup loosely packed watercress

Grate the zest of one of the oranges and reserve. Segment all three oranges (see Symon Says) and reserve with their juice.

In a large bowl, combine the garlic, shallot, salt, lemon zest and juice, and the orange zest and juice (reserve the segments for now), and whisk to combine. Add the shaved fennel, fennel fronds, and dill and toss them in the juices. Add the orange segments, a few grinds of black pepper, the coriander, extra-virgin olive oil, and watercress. Toss gently and divide the salad among four plates. Spoon additional dressing from the bottom of the bowl over each portion.

SYMON SAYS

Segmenting citrus fruits into what are called "supremes" allows you to serve them in an elegant way. To segment an orange or grapefruit, slice off the top and bottom of the rind. Then remove the rest of the rind, slicing from top to bottom, making sure to remove all the pith but leaving as much fruit as possible. When the fruit is peeled, slice through the fruit along either side of each membrane to remove only the fruit sections. Work over a bowl to capture the juices. When you have cut out all the segments, squeeze the remaining juice from the fruit into the bowl over the segments.

SLOW-ROASTED BEETS WITH BUTTERMILK BLUE CHEESE, WATERCRESS, AND TOASTED WALNUTS

I love using vegetables people don't think they like or didn't like as children, such as beets and Brussels sprouts, to show people how fantastic the vegetables can be when they're handled right. Beets especially are a great starter vegetable for kids because they're so sweet. When the spring and summer vegetables—fava beans, peas, corn, and tomatoes—have ended, that's when I turn to beets to fill the void; for me they're fall and winter vegetables.

This is a straightforward beet salad we've done since the original Lola: sweet roasted beets with peppery watercress, tangy blue cheese, and some crunch and nuttiness from walnuts, all tied together by a sweet and acidic vinaigrette using orange, honey, balsamic (the better your balsamic, the better your salad will be) and extra-virgin olive oil. With big vegetable salads like this, or with tomato salads, I like to serve lots of vinaigrette so that the salad is very juicy. Because the vinaigrette is not highly acidic, you can use it plentifully; the acidity of the cheese, Buttermilk Blue from Roth Käse in Wisconsin (see Sources, page 250), picks up the slack.

Serves 4 to 6

½ cup walnut pieces
Kosher salt
3 medium golden beets
3 medium red beets
1 head of garlic, halved through its
    equator
4 sprigs of fresh thyme
Freshly ground black pepper
1 shallot, minced

1 large garlic clove, minced
Grated zest and juice of 1 orange
1 tablespoon honey
1 tablespoon aged balsamic vinegar
¼ cup extra-virgin olive oil
4 ounces Roth Käse Buttermilk Blue or
    Maytag blue cheese, crumbled (1 cup)
1 cup loosely packed watercress

Preheat the oven to 400°F.

Spread out the walnuts on a rimmed baking sheet, sprinkle with a little salt, and toast in the oven until fragrant and lightly browned, 5 to 7 minutes. Set aside to cool.

Lower the oven temperature to 325°F. In a shallow baking dish large enough to accommodate all of the beets, place the golden and red beets, head of garlic, and thyme. Add enough water to reach ¼ inch up the sides of the pan. Season the beets with salt and pepper. Cover the pan snugly with foil and roast the beets until tender— a sharp knife will slide through to the center of each beet with little resistance when it's done—1 to 1½ hours. Remove the foil and allow the beets to cool. Trim the root and stem ends from the beets and peel them. Cut each beet into wedges.

In a large bowl, combine the shallot, minced garlic, a pinch of salt, the orange zest and juice, honey, and balsamic vinegar. Whisk to incorporate, check for seasoning, and add more salt if needed. Whisk in the extra-virgin olive oil. Add the beets, tossing gently to coat with vinaigrette. Taste again for seasoning and adjust if needed.

Divide the beets among four plates and top each portion with some of the toasted walnuts, crumbled blue cheese, and watercress. Drizzle with additional vinaigrette from the bottom of the bowl and finish with a few grinds of pepper.

TOMATO SALAD WITH RED ONION, DILL, AND FETA

Nothing gets me amped up like local heirloom tomatoes. It means summer is full on, and with summer comes rides on the Harley, golf, and this great salad. It's all about the tomato. Please be patient and wait until you can find tomatoes grown locally or, better yet, from your own garden. To put it bluntly, this is NOT a winter salad to be made with bland tomatoes shipped from halfway around the world that are red and round and taste like dry wall. Your patience will pay off. This dish can be served individually, but I prefer to put it on a platter to be served family style.

I love Mt. Vikos feta (see Sources, page 250), which is aged for four months in birch barrels and develops a rich flavor and creamy texture.

Serves 4

1 garlic clove, minced
Kosher salt
Freshly ground black pepper
¼ cup red wine vinegar
½ cup extra-virgin olive oil
½ red onion, shaved paper thin on a mandoline and soaked in ice water to cover for 10 minutes
1 red bell pepper, cored, seeded, and cut into 1-inch chunks

⅓ medium cucumber, thinly sliced
1 cup pitted whole kalamata olives
¼ cup coarsely chopped fresh dill
¼ cup coarsely chopped fresh mint
1 pound heirloom tomatoes (use an assortment of shapes, sizes, and colors), cut into bite-size chunks
1 cup crumbled barrel-aged feta

Combine the garlic, a pinch of salt, a grinding of pepper, and the vinegar in a large mixing bowl. Drizzle in the olive oil while whisking. Drain the onion, pat dry, and add to the bowl along with the bell pepper, cucumber, and olives. Let marinate for 15 to 20 minutes.

Add the dill, mint, tomatoes, and feta, and toss gently to combine. Season with salt and pepper to taste. Spoon onto a large platter and serve immediately.

SYMON SAYS

Store tomatoes at room temperature, never in the refrigerator—it kills their sweetness and makes them grainy. Cut tomatoes close to serving time so you don't lose a lot of their juices. If you buy too many, thinly slice them, sprinkle them with salt and thyme, and put on a cookie sheet. Dry them in a 150°F oven for 4 hours and they will keep for up to a month in the refrigerator.

ZUCCHINI CRUDO

This is a version of a salad Jonathan Waxman is known for and that I fell in love with when I first tasted it. Who'd have thought, after decades of cooking, that zucchini could be an epiphany. But it was. I simply never thought of eating it raw. Seriously, it was a jaw-dropping surprise. I think he dressed it only with salt, lemon, and olive oil. I've added some garlic and shallot—building the dressing on top of these raw aromatics—along with dill, because I love dill, and with almonds for crunch and nuttiness. It's important to salt the zucchini ten to fifteen minutes before serving it; this will leach out the right amount of water but leave some crunch. Put the salt on too early and you can lose that texture. If you need to prepare the dish ahead, the vinaigrette can be made up to a few hours in advance and you can slice the zucchini up to an hour before salting it if you cover it with a damp towel and leave it at room temperature.

Serves 4 to 6

2 zucchini (about ¾ pound), thinly sliced
2 yellow summer squash (about 1½ pounds), thinly sliced
1 tablespoon plus ¼ teaspoon kosher salt
1 teaspoon minced garlic
1 shallot, finely sliced

Grated zest and juice of 3 lemons, or to taste
½ cup extra-virgin olive oil
⅓ cup slivered or sliced almonds, toasted (see page 69)
⅓ cup chopped fresh dill

Combine the zucchini and yellow squash in a colander in the sink and sprinkle 1 tablespoon of the salt over it. Toss to coat, and set aside for 10 to 15 minutes, no longer. In a large bowl, combine the garlic and shallot, sprinkle with the remaining ¼ teaspoon salt, and whisk in the lemon zest and juice. Whisk in the olive oil in a steady stream, then the almonds and dill. Taste for seasoning and acidity (it should be nicely acidic).

Add the zucchini and squash to the dressing, toss, and serve immediately.

Pasta, Gnocchi, and Risotto

At my restaurants, and traditionally in Italy, pasta dishes are starting courses. They're smaller; they lead into the meal. But let's face it, there's something incredibly satisfying about sitting down and eating a giant bowl of pasta as a meal. Maybe a little salad, some crusty bread, some wine.

Fresh pasta is rich and delicious just as it is. You can serve it as a starter, you can serve it as a main course, you can serve it family style. And once you realize how easy it is to make a basic dough, you can make so many things—noodles, spaghetti, ravioli, lasagna. Because the shaping, topping, and filling combinations are endless, pasta is a staple that extends your range in the kitchen.

Gnocchi works in the same way pasta does, carrying any number of garnishes, but I think it works especially well with vegetables. I respect risotto so much that I don't serve it at the restaurant. It's not difficult, but I don't believe you can par-cook it, and I'm not set up to do it properly in a restaurant setting. Risotto requires commitment from the cook to take it from start to finish, so I only make it at home, where it is nothing but a pleasure.

Fresh Pasta

There should be no reason why you can't make fresh pasta a routine in your kitchen. My recipe for pasta dough requires virtually no kneading, so it's especially quick and easy. It is an all-yolk recipe that results in a very rich, flavorful pasta that, as a result of the minimal kneading, has a very tender bite.

Flour is important. I use Italian "00" flour, which is increasingly available here in Italian markets. In Italy, flour is rated according to how finely ground it is, with "00" being the finest. It's principally used in making pizza dough and pasta, and it is worth seeking out, either locally or online, though all-purpose flour can be substituted. I add a little salt and a little olive oil for flavor—that's it.

The way I learned pasta—the way so many books teach pasta—is that the dough must be kneaded for ten minutes or so until it is as soft as a baby's tush. The reasoning is that the gluten, which is the protein in flour, must line up neatly to give you elasticity in your dough so that it can be rolled out well. With my quick-knead method, though, you let the rollers of the pasta machine do the kneading for you instead. (While pasta dough can be rolled out on a work surface using a rolling pin, I don't recommend rolling this dough by hand; pasta rollers start at a little more than twenty dollars, so it's not really a huge investment for fresh pasta.)

The thickness of the pasta depends on the type of pasta you're making. For the wide noodle, pappardelle, and for linguine, I finish the pasta on the second to last setting on the pasta rollers for noodles with a little heft. For ravioli, I like to finish it on the thinnest setting.

To prevent it from sticking, I toss the cut pasta with rice flour, a very fine flour that has relatively little gluten and so won't make the pasta tough; but Wondra flour is fine to use.

To cook pasta, the most important step is to season your water properly. This does not mean putting a pinch of salt in a big pot of water. It means adding enough salt that the water tastes seasoned, so that the water has the same seasoning level you want your finished pasta to have. I use about 3 tablespoons kosher salt per gallon. Allow your water to return to a rapid boil—there should be plenty of water—and cook the pasta to al dente, so that it has some bite to it.

When you drain it, reserve some of the water to thin your sauce if necessary. Do not rinse your pasta! You'll wash away the starch, which allows the sauce to cling to your pasta.

EGG YOLK PASTA DOUGH

This quick-knead dough is a summary of my pasta convictions. Except for the mac and cheese on page 89, which uses dried pasta, all of the pasta recipes in this book use this fresh dough.

Makes 1 pound dough, enough to serve 4 to 6

1½ cups (7 ounces) "00" or all-purpose
  flour
½ teaspoon kosher salt
9 large egg yolks

1 teaspoon extra-virgin olive oil
Rice flour or Wondra flour, as needed for
  dusting the cut pasta

Mound the "00" flour on a cutting board or countertop. Sprinkle the salt over it. Form a well in the center of the flour and pour in the yolks. Add the olive oil and break each yolk. Using a plastic bench scraper (my tool of choice) or your fingers, draw the flour over the yolks from the perimeter. Continue to mix the flour into the yolks until it's all incorporated, kneading only enough for it to come together. Shape it into a rectangle about ½ inch thick. The mixture should be dense, flaky, and crumbly. Cover the dough with a damp towel and let it rest for 10 to 30 minutes.

Cut the dough into four pieces. Take one piece of dough (keeping the others covered) and flatten it with your hands. If the dough feels very dry, dampen the surface with a few drops of water using your fingers or a pastry brush. Starting with the rollers of your pasta machine set to the widest setting, pass the dough through, five or six times, or until the dough begins to become pliable. Do the same for the remaining pieces. Narrow the rollers by one setting and roll each piece through it once. Continue narrowing the rollers and rolling the pasta through each consecutive setting one time until the dough has reached the desired thickness.

Proceed to cut the pasta as desired, tossing the finished pasta with rice flour to prevent sticking. Pasta at this point can sit at room temperature covered with parchment or a dry towel, something that will allow it to breathe but not dry out, for up to half a day. It can also be cut as desired, tossed with rice flour, and frozen in plastic bags for up to a month. There's no need to thaw it before you want to cook it.

LINGUINE WITH HEIRLOOM TOMATO, CAPERS, ANCHOVIES, AND CHILE

This simple tomato-based pasta dish originated because one of my chefs, Jonathon Sawyer, now chef of a nearby restaurant in Cleveland, loved loved loved anchovies. He used to put them in everything, using them almost like an aromatic or an herb. I love fresh anchovies, fried, but I've never been a fan of whole cured or canned anchovies, such as anchovies on a pizza. But they are a great seasoning device and I love working them into sauces; it's a quick, easy way to punch up the flavor.

I urge you to make your own linguine for this one because otherwise the dish is almost too easy, but if you're pressed for time, some dried pasta will work fine too.

Serves 4 to 6

Kosher salt
1 cup dried bread crumbs, preferably homemade
1 tablespoon olive oil
3 garlic cloves, sliced
1 teaspoon crushed red pepper flakes
Egg Yolk Pasta Dough (page 83), rolled and cut into linguine

1 large brandywine heirloom tomato, peeled, seeded, and diced (1 cup)
6 salt-packed anchovies, rinsed, filleted, and minced
1 tablespoon salt-packed capers, rinsed and patted dry
¼ cup extra-virgin olive oil
¼ cup sliced fresh flat-leaf parsley leaves

Bring a pot of water to a boil for the pasta and add salt until it tastes seasoned. Toast the bread crumbs in a dry skillet over medium heat, tossing as needed, until lightly browned, about 3 or 4 minutes. Remove from the heat.

Heat the olive oil in a large sauté pan over medium heat. When the oil is hot, add the garlic and sweat it for 2 minutes. Add the red pepper flakes and cook for another 30 seconds.

Drop the pasta in the boiling water and cook until al dente, about 2 minutes.

Meanwhile, add the tomato, anchovies, and capers to the sauté pan, bring to a simmer, and cook for 2 minutes, or until the tomato has released its juices and the anchovies have melted into the sauce. Remove the sauce from the heat and add the extra-virgin olive oil and parsley.

Strain the pasta and add it directly to the sauce. Toss well before dividing among four bowls. Top with the bread crumbs.

SHEEP'S-MILK RAVIOLI WITH BROWN BUTTER AND ALMONDS

On special occasions my yia yia (my Greek grandma) would make ricotta ravioli. It was a tradition that went away as she got older, and she passed away without any of us having written down her recipe. So this is my version of a family tradition, and it's a dish that we often serve at Lolita. I season ricotta with abundant orange zest, salt, and pepper for the filling and serve the finished ravioli with a simple brown butter sauce. Make the extra effort to find sheep's-milk ricotta as it really is the star of this pasta—it has more body to it, a little tang. If you can't find sheep's-milk ricotta, mix some fresh goat cheese into cow's-milk ricotta to give it more depth.

Serves 4

Ravioli
1 cup sheep's-milk ricotta
½ cup grated Parmesan cheese
1 large egg
Grated zest of 1 orange
½ teaspoon kosher salt, plus more for
    pasta water

¼ teaspoon freshly ground black pepper
Egg Yolk Pasta Dough (page 83)
Rice flour or Wondra flour, for the work
    surface

Sauce
12 tablespoons (1½ sticks) unsalted
    butter
¼ cup sliced almonds

Grated zest and juice of ½ orange
¼ cup chopped fresh flat-leaf parsley
    leaves

To make the filling for the ravioli, put the ricotta in a fine-mesh strainer set over a bowl and let drain in the refrigerator overnight.

Dump the ricotta into a large bowl, discarding the drained liquid. Stir in the Parmesan, egg, orange zest, salt, and pepper. Cover and refrigerate while preparing the pasta sheets.

Roll the 4 pieces of dough through the first setting of your machine. They should each measure about 4 to 5 inches wide and 18 inches long. Lay out the sheets of dough on a countertop dusted with flour. Along one long half of each sheet of pasta, place four 2-teaspoon-size dollops of filling. Moisten the edges of the pasta with water, fold the unfilled side of the dough over the filling side, and press around the perimeter of each mound to seal. Using a round ravioli or 2-inch cookie or biscuit cutter, cut out the ravioli and place on a floured rimmed baking sheet. You should have 12 to 16 ravioli. You can wrap and refrigerate the ravioli at this point for up to a day or freeze for 1 month.

Bring a large pot of water to a boil, and add enough salt so that it tastes seasoned. When the water returns to a boil, add the ravioli and boil until they float. Once they float, cook for 1 minute longer.

While the ravioli are cooking, make the sauce. Heat the butter over medium-high heat in a sauté pan large enough to later accommodate the cooked ravioli. When the butter is foaming, add the sliced almonds and sauté until golden brown, about 2 minutes.

Scoop the ravioli from the cooking water with a slotted spoon, leaving excess water clinging to the pasta (this helps form the sauce), and transfer to the sauté pan along with the orange juice. Toss once or twice until the contents of the pan are well acclimated.

Remove the pan from the heat, add the parsley and orange zest, and divide among four shallow bowls, spooning sauce and garnish over the ravioli.

PAPPARDELLE WITH PIG'S-HEAD RAGÙ

At Lolita we often get in whole hogs to make our charcuterie. Now I like head-cheese as much as the next guy, but what I like even more is slowly cooking the head in some of my Yia Yia's Sunday Sauce. The head gives the sauce incredible body, and the picked meat is super-tender and loaded with flavor. The biggest bonus is the shriek of the vegetarian servers or of children when they sneak a peak at what I've got cooking, only to be stared down by the head of the hog. Now that's good American fun! If you don't want to use a whole pig's head, you can use 1½ pounds pork shoulder cut into large dice combined with a couple of pig's trotters for the gelatin in the skin, roasted as instructed for the pig's head.

Serves 8

1 head from a 12- to 18-pound suckling
    pig
Kosher salt
Yia Yia's Sunday Sauce (page 229)
1½ cups red wine

1 tablespoon crushed red pepper flakes
1 bay leaf
Egg Yolk Pasta Dough (page 83)
Rice flour or Wondra flour, for dusting the
    cut pasta

Preheat the oven to 375°F.

Season the pig's head with salt and roast in a roasting pan in the oven for 1 hour.

Transfer the head to a large pot and add the sauce, wine, red pepper flakes, and bay leaf. Bring to a simmer over very low heat and cook for 3 hours, skimming away excess fat. Turn off the heat under the sauce. Remove the head from the sauce and let it cool.

Roll the pasta in a pasta roller going all the way to the second to thinnest setting. Dust the pasta sheets with flour, then fold each sheet in half lengthwise and then in half again, and place on a lightly floured cutting board. With a sharp knife, cut the pasta into ½- to ¾-inch-wide noodles, tossing with more flour if necessary. Cover with parchment paper or a dry kitchen towel.

Pull all the meat from the head and coarsely chop the meat, saving any excess skin.

Crisp the skin in a hot dry sauté pan over high heat, turning once, about 1 minute. Return the skin and the meat to the sauce. Return the sauce to a simmer. Discard the bay leaf before serving.

Bring a large pot of water to a boil, and add enough salt so that it tastes seasoned. When the water returns to a boil, cook the pappardelle until al dente, 1 to 2 minutes. Drain and toss with about half of the sauce.

MAC AND CHEESE WITH ROASTED CHICKEN, GOAT CHEESE, AND ROSEMARY

This is my stepson Kyle's favorite dish ever—and I urge parents to try this for your kids who are picky. The dish had an almost instant cult-like following from the day I put it on the menu at Piccolo Mondo in 1992, and to this day, I can't take it off the menu. It's comfort food times ten, delicious, a great way to use leftover roast chicken—a dish that's special enough for entertaining and easy enough for a quick Sunday night dinner. The only thing that upsets me about this dish is that it's the only thing Kyle will eat when he goes to the restaurant. And he's not a *kid* anymore.

This is a dish that breaks a few primary rules: it pairs rich with rich, and the textures are soft on soft. But it is deeply satisfying.

Serves 6 to 8

Kosher salt
1 pound dried rigatoni pasta
1 quart (4 cups) heavy cream

2 tablespoons chopped fresh rosemary
8 ounces fresh goat cheese (1 cup)
2 cups shredded roasted chicken

Bring a large pot of water to a boil, and add enough salt so that it tastes seasoned. While the water is coming to a boil, put the cream, rosemary, and ½ teaspoon salt in a large saucepan over high heat. Bring just to a simmer, then lower the heat to medium and simmer to reduce the mixture by half.

Add the goat cheese and chicken to the cream and bring the mixture back to a simmer. Continue cooking until it coats the back of a spoon, about 30 minutes.

Add the rigatoni to the boiling water and cook it until al dente, about 10 minutes. Drain the pasta from the water and add to the sauce. Toss the pasta to combine it with the sauce and bring it back just to a simmer.

SYMON SAYS

Be careful heating cream. When it comes to a boil it will quickly climb the sides of the pot and boil over. If you're not careful your stove will be a mess and you won't have enough cream in your pot, so pay attention during the initial heating of the cream.

RISOTTO WITH BAY SCALLOPS

I used to serve risotto at Lola—and then I got smart. It's got to be done all at once, and you've got to stir constantly. For these reasons, it doesn't make sense for me to do it at a restaurant unless I want to cook it to order, which just isn't practical for us.

But I do love to cook risotto at home; that's where I give it the attention it deserves. It's so soul-satisfying to make and to serve and to eat. And it's really easy. It does take patience, however. But, again, this is why I love it: it's a commitment dish. It's not like you can just throw it in a pan and walk away. The key is stirring the rice to release all the starch that makes it creamy and delicious. Keep it simple: sweat garlic and onion in olive oil, add the rice and toast it, then add your wine, cook it down, add some stock, cook it down, add more stock, stirring pretty much continuously until it's just tender, and finish it with some cheese and a little butter. That's it. I do think it's a preparation that requires fresh stock. Water just doesn't have the flavor or body, and inferior canned broths reduce, thereby intensifying their inferior flavor.

Serves 4

2 tablespoons olive oil
1 medium yellow onion, minced
2 garlic cloves, minced
½ cup diced prosciutto
1 cup Arborio rice
1 generous pinch of saffron
½ cup dry white wine

3 to 4 cups Chicken Stock (page 131), warmed
½ pound bay scallops, or ½ pound sea scallops cut into ½-inch pieces
¼ cup sliced fresh flat-leaf parsley leaves
1 tablespoon unsalted butter
2 tablespoons grated Parmesan

Heat the olive oil in a 4-quart saucepan over medium heat. Add the onion and sweat it for 2 minutes. Add the garlic and sweat it for 2 minutes more. Add the prosciutto and cook it until it crisps, about 1 minute. Add the rice and let it toast slightly in the hot fat, about 1 minute, stirring with a wooden spoon.

Reduce the heat to low, add the saffron and wine, and stir continuously until most of the wine has cooked off. Add 1 cup of the stock and stir continuously until the liquid has cooked off, about 3 minutes. Add another cup of stock and repeat the process. Taste the rice. Continue to add stock in ¼-cup increments until the rice is tender and the risotto is creamy.

Add the scallops and continue to stir for 2 minutes, or until the scallops are heated through. Remove the pan from the heat and stir in the parsley, butter, and cheese and serve immediately.

CRISPY GNOCCHI WITH MORELS AND SPRING PEAS

After the endless winter in Cleveland, nothing is more exciting for us than spring and all the food that begins to grow. Local morel mushrooms and fresh English peas start to pop up at markets. And that's when I make these flour-and-ricotta gnocchi. We make and serve potato gnocchi at the restaurants, but I prefer potato gnocchi with meat and fish or heavy ragùs, and I love these with vegetables.

I first had these gnocchi at Jonathan Waxman's restaurant Barbuto in New York City and they were so good that I asked him how he had made them. He said, "You're welcome to steal them from me, but you gotta figure out how to make them yourself!" So I came back and played around with the dough until I came up with this. The dough is actually not the thing—I'd made tons of ricotta gnocchi before. But I'd always boiled them, so they came out soft. When you sauté them in brown butter instead, they crisp up and become a completely different food. (Remember that you need to drain your ricotta for at least a few hours or overnight.)

Serves 4

Gnocchi
¾ cup (3½ ounces) all-purpose flour, plus more for dusting
½ cup grated Parmesan cheese
Grated zest of 1 lemon
¼ teaspoon kosher salt
1 cup whole-milk ricotta, drained (see page 86)
1 large egg

Sauce
8 tablespoons (1 stick) unsalted butter
12 medium morels, soaked briefly in salted water, rinsed, and gently patted dry
½ shallot, thinly sliced
Kosher salt
1 garlic clove, thinly sliced
12 fresh flat-leaf parsley leaves
Juice of 1 lemon
½ cup shelled fresh peas
⅓ cup grated Parmesan cheese

For the gnocchi dough, combine the flour, Parmesan, lemon zest, and salt in a bowl. Add the ricotta and egg. Combine well with a wooden spoon or your fingers until the dough just comes together, taking care not to overwork, which could cause the dough to toughen.

Scrape the dough onto a well-floured work surface and pat into a rough square. Cut the dough into thirds using a bench scraper or knife. Gently roll each piece into foot-long ropes, about an inch in diameter, flouring as needed to prevent the dough

recipe continued on next page

from sticking to the surface. Place the dough ropes onto a lightly floured plate or rimmed baking sheet and refrigerate, uncovered, for 5 minutes and up to 2 hours.

After the dough has rested, return the ropes to a floured surface. Cut each rope into ½-inch pieces with a bench scraper or knife and set aside while you start the sauce.

Put 4 tablespoons of the butter in a medium sauté pan over medium-high heat. When the butter foams, add the morels and sauté until they begin to soften, about 2 minutes. Add the shallot and sauté, seasoning with a pinch of salt. Add the garlic and parsley, then reduce the heat to medium. Add the lemon juice and peas, sauté-ing just until the peas brighten in color. Turn off the heat and set aside while you sauté the gnocchi.

Heat 3 tablespoons of the butter over medium-high heat in a sauté pan large enough to accommodate all of the gnocchi without crowding. When the butter becomes brown and fragrant, add the gnocchi to the pan and cook, turning as necessary, until they're browned and crisp on all sides, 5 or 6 minutes. Pour in the morel and pea sauce, turning to coat. Add the remaining tablespoon butter, the Parmesan, and 2 tablespoons of water while turning the gnocchi. Allow the sauce ingredients to emulsify and form a silken coating, 1 to 2 minutes. Spoon the gnocchi and sauce into shallow bowls and serve immediately.

Charcuterie

While it's enjoying something of a renaissance in America, especially among restaurant chefs, charcuterie—a category of cooking that applies primarily to cured or cooked meats and dry-cured, cooked, and fresh sausages—is still a dying art in my mind because it's so infrequently practiced at home. Most people still go out and buy bacon and salami rather than attempt to make their own. This is a crying shame because there are just so many things to be learned from the craft of charcuterie, so much flavor to be created, so much pleasure in the making and the eating.

As a chef, my love of charcuterie runs deep. There's something truly satisfying about taking cheaper cuts of meat and off cuts and turning them into something spectacular, which is really what charcuterie is about. The most important part of practicing charcuterie for me is that it allows me to control the flavors of my dishes from start to finish, whether it's adding coriander and dried chili to the bacon cure, controlling the fat content in a sausage, or choosing the breed of hog that gives me the best belly for curing, and how much smoke to give it.

Charcuterie takes time and thought and therefore encourages a respect for our food.

A word about an ingredient generically referred to as pink salt. Pink salt refers to sodium nitrite, a curing salt that's dyed pink. It gives a piquant flavor to products like ham and bacon, keeps the meat pink, and protects it from the bacterium that causes botulism (important especially in smoked foods and dry-cured sausages). Pink salt is sold under different names and is available by mail from butcher-packer.com, which sells it under the name DQ Curing Salt.

LOLA BACON AND LOLITA PANCETTA

When pork belly is cured and smoked it's called bacon. When it's cured and dried but not smoked, it's called pancetta. Following are the recipes we use at the restaurants for both preparations. Bacon is by definition hot smoked, that is, smoked and cooked (we use an Alto-Shaam smoker), but there's no reason you can't use the bacon cure and then cook the belly in a 200°F oven until it reaches a temperature of 150°F, then cool and refrigerate it. This still results in delicious "bacon."

Our bacon takes on a little bit of spice from dried chili; savory notes from paprika and cumin; and sweetness from brown sugar and honey. I prefer to use bellies from Duroc hogs, a heritage breed that's coming back, for their high proportion of fat to meat, but any belly can be used. Just remember: the more fat, the more flavor!

If you don't have the ability or inclination to smoke foods but you still want to cure your own bacon, you can try the dry-cured pancetta. It's often rolled into a log to dry, but we dry it flat because it's faster. For the pancetta, the cure takes ten to twelve days, and the drying takes about three weeks. No matter how you're preparing the belly keep in mind that it must cure for at least seven days in the refrigerator; and if you plan to smoke it, you'll need to let it dry for another two days.

LOLA BACON

Makes 3½ pounds

5 pounds pork belly, skin on
¼ cup kosher salt
2 teaspoons pink salt (see page 97)
¼ cup packed dark brown sugar

¼ cup honey, preferably chestnut honey
2 tablespoons crushed red pepper flakes
2 tablespoons smoked sweet paprika
1 teaspoon cumin seeds

Rinse the pork belly and pat dry. Transfer to a 2-gallon resealable plastic bag.

Mix the kosher salt, pink salt, brown sugar, honey, red pepper flakes, paprika, and cumin. Coat the belly all over with the mixture. Close the bag and refrigerate for 7 to 10 days, flipping once a day, until the belly feels firm (7 days for a thin belly, about 1½ inches, longer for a belly that's 2 to 3 inches thick).

Remove the belly from the bag, rinse thoroughly, and pat dry. Refrigerate the belly on a rack, uncovered, for 48 hours.

Set up your smoker according to the manufacturer's instructions and using apple wood chips and set to 200°F. Smoke the belly for 3 hours, or until the bacon reaches an internal temperature of 150°F. Slice the rind off, leaving as much fat on the bacon as possible. Wrap in plastic wrap and refrigerate for 1 week or freeze for up to 2 months.

LOLITA PANCETTA

Makes 3½ pounds

5 pounds pork belly with skin cut off
¼ cup kosher salt
2 teaspoons pink salt (see page 97)
3 tablespoons packed dark brown sugar
4 garlic cloves, minced

2 tablespoons chopped fresh rosemary
1 tablespoon crushed red pepper flakes
4 bay leaves, crumbled
2 tablespoons cracked black pepper

Rinse the pork belly and pat dry. Transfer the belly to a 2-gallon resealable plastic bag.

Mix the kosher salt, pink salt, brown sugar, garlic, rosemary, red pepper flakes, bay leaves, and black pepper. Coat the belly all over with the mixture. Close the bag and refrigerate for 10 to 12 days, flipping once a day.

Remove the belly from the bag, rinse thoroughly, and pat dry. Weigh the cured belly and record the weight. Hang the belly (punch a hole in one end and thread butcher's string through it) or set it on a rack and turn it every so often in a cool dark place (ideally at 55°F at 60 percent humidity) for 3 weeks.

Weigh the belly. The belly should have lost 30 percent of its weight. (If it hasn't, let it hang until it does, testing every few days.) Wrap well in plastic and refrigerate until ready to use. It will keep this way for up to a month.

SYMON SAYS

Don't throw pig skin away! It's loaded with collagen, which gives body to stocks and stews. Add it to a pot of beans for great flavor and body. At the restaurant, we confit it (follow the instructions on page 38 for confiting the pig's ears, after they've been cured), then slice it in half-inch strips and fry them as cracklings to garnish salads.

LAMB BRESAOLA

Perhaps the easiest things to dry-cure at home are whole muscles. Bresaola typically refers to beef loin that's been dry-cured, but I love to dry-cure lamb. You can use either a boneless cut from the leg or a lamb loin. It results in a beautiful intensely lamby flavor. Serve it shaved paper thin with crusty bread, some arugula, and olive oil.

Makes 1½ pounds

2 pounds lamb loin or leg
2 tablespoons kosher salt
2 tablespoons sugar
½ teaspoon pink salt (see page 97)

2 tablespoons chopped fresh rosemary
1 teaspoon chopped fresh lavender
1 teaspoon freshly ground black pepper

Rinse the lamb and pat dry. Transfer to a 2-gallon resealable plastic bag.

Mix the kosher salt, sugar, pink salt, rosemary, lavender, and black pepper. Coat the lamb all over with the mixture. Close the bag and refrigerate for 7 to 10 days, flipping once a day.

Remove the lamb from the bag, rinse thoroughly, and pat dry. Weigh the cured lamb and record the weight. Hang the lamb in a cool dark place (ideally 55°F at 60 percent humidity) for 3 to 4 weeks.

Weigh the lamb. The lamb should have lost 30 percent of its weight. (If it hasn't, let it hang until it does, testing every few days.) Wrap well in plastic and refrigerate until ready to use. It will keep this way for up to a month.

Fresh Sausages

Fresh sausage and pasta are my two favorite items to make. They're therapeutic. So many things you do in a restaurant you rush through; you've got so much going on you can't take the time you need to really appreciate what you're doing. You can't do that with sausage; you *have* to take your time. It's not as hard as you may think, especially if you stay organized. Good planning, good preparation, and taking your time make sausage making fun.

I love the technical aspect of it. Sausage making isn't difficult, but a few parts of the process require special attention. Seasoning a day ahead I think is absolutely essential, in both whole muscles and in diced meat and fat that will be ground; it deepens the flavor and gives the finished sausage a more pleasing texture. Temperature also affects texture. The meat and the fat must always be kept very cold (this can't be overstated). And finally, you've got to achieve the correct ratio of fat to meat to end up with juicy—not dry—sausages.

Sausage making is the greatest skill I learned from Carl Quagliata, legendary Cleveland restaurateur and one of my mentors. Carl's father was a butcher here, and Carl is master of everything ground and stuffed.

I use fresh sausage in many ways at home and on my menus. When I go to a restaurant I'm always more impressed with a grilled sausage than with a grilled piece of beef tenderloin with a fancy sauce. Loose sausage is the easiest way to put your homemade versions to use; I stuff peppers with it (see page 32) and use it crumbled and cooked as the main flavoring agent in a sauce for scallops (it makes a great sauce for all shellfish). If you stuff it into casing for links, you can serve it in a sandwich, on its own with a simple sauce, or as a starting course, with a little salad. A lamb sausage, for example, is great with a dollop of Greek yogurt and a pile of shaved fennel and bell peppers with mint and a lemon vinaigrette.

Here are three different sausages, made from three different meats, with three different flavor profiles: pork (sweet and garlicky), veal (spicy with Italian seasoning), and lamb (spicy in the style of merguez).

PORK SAUSAGE

Makes 2 pounds, or about 8 6-inch links; serves 6 to 8

1½ pounds pork shoulder, diced
½ pound pork fatback, diced
1 tablespoon sugar
1 tablespoon kosher salt
3 garlic cloves, minced

1½ teaspoons fennel seeds, toasted (see
    Symon Says, page 69)
4 feet of hog casings (optional), soaked in
    water for at least 30 minutes and then
    flushed with water

Combine the meat, fatback, sugar, salt, garlic, and fennel seeds in a bowl. Cover and refrigerate overnight.

About 30 minutes before grinding, place all the equipment in the freezer to get cold.

Grind the sausage mixture through a small die and return it to the refrigerator to cool for 30 minutes.

Using the paddle attachment on your mixer, mix the sausage on low speed for 30 seconds. Raise the speed to medium and add 6 tablespoons cold water. Mix for another minute or two to bring everything together.

At this point you have three options. You can stuff it into casings, form it into patties, or crumble it. The sausage will keep for up to 1 week covered in the refrigerator, or freeze for up to a month. Cook to an internal temperature of 150°F before serving.

SYMON SAYS

If you find yourself making sausage often, it's worth investing in a five-pound cylindrical stuffer with a crank handle (see Sources, page 250). While the grinder attachment to your standing mixer is fine, I don't recommend the stuffer attachment that is also available. Most are messy, inconvenient, and don't create the right interior texture.

VEAL SAUSAGE

Makes 2 pounds, or about 8 6-inch links; serves 6 to 8

4 garlic cloves, minced
½ cup minced shallot
2 teaspoons olive oil
1½ pounds veal shoulder, trimmed and
    cubed
½ pound pork fatback, cubed
1 tablespoon crushed red pepper flakes
2 tablespoons fennel seeds, toasted (see
    Symon Says, page 69)

2 tablespoons coriander seeds, toasted
    and ground (page 69; about
    1½ tablespoons)
1 tablespoon kosher salt
1 teaspoon sugar
4 feet of hog casings (optional), soaked in
    water for at least 30 minutes
    and then flushed with water

Sweat the garlic and shallot over medium-low heat in a sauté pan with the olive oil until translucent, about 2 minutes. Remove from the heat and let cool completely.

Remove the cubed meat and fatback from the refrigerator and combine it in a large bowl with the shallot mixture, red pepper flakes, fennel seeds, coriander, salt, and sugar. Toss well to combine. Cover the mixture and refrigerate it for 24 hours.

About 30 minutes before grinding, place all the equipment in the freezer to get cold.

Grind the sausage mixture twice through a medium die or small die and return it to the refrigerator to cool for 30 minutes.

Using the paddle attachment on your mixer, mix the sausage on medium speed for 45 to 60 seconds, to bring everything together. At this point you have three options. You can stuff it into casings, form it into patties, or crumble it. The sausage will keep for up to 1 week covered in the refrigerator, or freeze for up to a month. Cook to an internal temperature of 150°F before serving.

SYMON SAYS

I can't stress enough how important it is to keep everything cold. If the meat and fat get warm during the grinding or mixing process, you will end up with a grainy sausage. So take the extra time to make sure that the meat itself and anything it comes in contact with is chilled.

LAMB SAUSAGE

Makes 2 pounds, or about 8 6-inch links; serves 6 to 8

1 garlic clove, minced
¼ cup minced shallot
½ tablespoon olive oil
1½ pounds lamb shoulder, cubed
½ pound pork fatback, cubed
2 teaspoons smoked sweet paprika
½ tablespoon cayenne pepper
¾ teaspoon cumin seeds, toasted and
  ground (see Symon Says, page 69;
  ½ teaspoon)

1 teaspoon ancho chili powder
1 tablespoon kosher salt
½ teaspoon sugar
4 feet of hog casings (optional), soaked in
  water for at least 30 minutes and then
  flushed with water

Sweat the garlic and shallot over medium heat in a sauté pan with the olive oil until translucent, about 2 minutes. Remove from the heat and let cool completely.

Remove the cubed meat and fatback from the refrigerator and combine it in a large bowl with the shallot mixture, paprika, cayenne pepper, cumin, chili powder, salt, and sugar. Toss well to combine. Cover the mixture and refrigerate it for 24 hours.

About 30 minutes before grinding, place all the equipment in the freezer to get cold.

Grind the sausage mixture twice through a medium die or small die and return it to the refrigerator to cool for 30 minutes.

Using the paddle attachment on your mixer, mix the sausage on medium speed for 45 to 60 seconds, to bring everything together.

At this point you have three options. You can stuff it into casings, form it into patties, or crumble it. The sausage will keep for up to 1 week covered in the refrigerator, or freeze for up to 1 month. Cook to an internal temperature of 150°F before serving.

POACHED FOIE GRAS BRATWURST

This is a more complex, more expensive sausage than the other recipes in the book (though it's not more difficult). An emulsified sausage—the ground meat and fat are puréed for a uniform and smooth texture—it's probably most geared to restaurant chefs and ambitious home cooks because it requires a few extra steps. It's a great sausage to make if your restaurant uses foie gras, because you might have a lot of trimmings to make use of. I created it for a dish called Picnic in Cleveland and served the sausage on grilled brioche with mustard and with Turnip Kraut (page 126). The industry magazine *Food Arts* recently chose it as one of their favorite recipes.

Makes about 2 pounds, or 16 to 20 4-inch links; serves 8 to 10

Foie Gras Bratwurst
¾ pound pork jowl, diced
½ pound veal shoulder, diced
2 tablespoons kosher salt
1 tablespoon ground white pepper
2 teaspoons smoked sweet paprika
1 teaspoon pink salt (see page 97)
½ teaspoon ground mace
½ teaspoon grated nutmeg

½ teaspoon ground cloves
½ pound foie gras, cold
1 cup whole milk, frozen and cut into cubes
2 large egg whites, beaten until frothy
4 feet of hog casings, soaked in water for at least 30 minutes and then flushed with water

Poaching Stock
1 gallon Chicken Stock (page 131) or water
1 medium onion, chopped

2 bunches of fresh marjoram
¼ cup kosher salt
2 garlic cloves, peeled

To make the bratwurst, in a large bowl, combine the pork jowl, veal shoulder, kosher salt, white pepper, paprika, pink salt, mace, nutmeg, and cloves. Cover with plastic wrap and refrigerate for 12 to 24 hours.

Transfer the meat mixture to the freezer for 30 minutes, or until it is stiff but not frozen solid.

About 30 minutes before grinding, place all the equipment in the freezer.

Grind the meat mixture twice through a medium die or small die. Repeat with the foie gras, grinding through the same die. Cover and refrigerate separately for 30 minutes.

Put the ground meat in the bowl of a food processor with half of the frozen milk cubes and purée until smooth. Add the foie gras and remaining milk and purée until the foie gras is incorporated. Put the sausage mixture in a bowl set in an ice bath and then fold in the egg whites.

recipe continued on next page

Stuff the casings and tie off with twine at 4-inch intervals.

To make the poaching liquid, combine the stock, onion, marjoram, salt, and garlic in a large pot and bring to a simmer. Cook for 30 minutes. Allow the poaching liquid to cool to 180°F; return the pot to low heat to maintain this temperature. Put the sausages into the poaching liquid and weight them down with a plate to ensure that they're completely submerged. Cook until they reach an internal temperature of 150°F, 10 to 15 minutes. Remove the sausages to an ice bath and chill thoroughly.

Reheat gently in a sauté pan to serve, or you can slice them and serve them cold.

Confit

Perhaps the easiest way to preserve meat at home is to confit it; typically duck, goose, or pork is briefly cured with salt and seasonings, cooked very gently for hours and hours—submerged in its own fat—and then cooled and chilled in the fat. The meat can then be reheated and the skin crisped for the most deeply seasoned, soul-satisfying, succulent morsels you've ever tasted.

Why is it so valuable to the cook? First, it's one of those techniques that allows you to take a tough inexpensive or off cut of meat and transform it into a great dish. It allows you to infuse the meat with extraordinary flavor through the cure. The cooking method results in meat that is the ultimate in rich unctuousness. And it only gets better the longer you keep it submerged in the fat, its flavors deepening with time.

Meat that has been confited, no matter the cut, can be used in many ways. It's delicious on its own, with some bread and mustard, as a kind of canapé. But it also makes a powerful main course. It goes beautifully with lean acidic components, which is why it's so often paired with salads. It's so tender that you can shred it and use it as a stuffing. And it makes a fantastic supporting player, to garnish a lean main course, for example. The Scallops with Lamb Sausage and Beans on page 178 would also go well with most confits—lamb, duck, or pork.

At the restaurant we use duck fat and lard for confiting, but there's no reason you can't confit in olive oil (and you will have some really delicious olive oil for drizzling when you're finished).

The first step is a one-day cure. I'm using duck here, but all meats go through pretty much the same steps. The only thing that differs is the cure recipe. For duck I use salt, sugar, cinnamon, coriander, paprika, bay leaves, garlic, and shallot; but you can tailor the seasoning to suit your taste. Add more sweet spices such as allspice and nutmeg, or make it spicy with dried chilies.

After the cure, the meat is rinsed and patted dry, submerged in the fat, and popped in a low oven, 200°F, for 8 to 10 hours. The meat is then removed from the oven, and when it's cool enough, it's refrigerated. And that's it. The hardest part of the method is not eating this fantastic meat as soon as it's out of the oven! But I think it really deserves to be left to "ripen," as it's often called, for at least five days. Or longer. If the meat is properly stored and completely submerged there's no reason you can't keep a confit refrigerated for several months.

DUCK CONFIT

Duck is readily available and rich tasting, so that's my choice here. Duck fat is very flavorful so that's the best fat to use, though you can use lard or even olive oil (but solid fat works as a more efficient preservative). Duck fat can be found in gourmet stores, online, and at Whole Foods.

Feature duck confit on the bone with crispy skin over a salad. Or you can cook it with beans (it's a main ingredient in cassoulet, the French legume stew). Or pull it off the bone and use it as you wish, on spicy greens, or as a filling for ravioli (see page 86), pierogies (see page 45), or corn crêpes (see page 40).

Serves 8

8 duck legs and thighs
3 tablespoons kosher salt
1 teaspoon sugar
1 tablespoon coriander seeds, toasted and crushed (see Symon Says, page 69)

1 teaspoon ground cinnamon
1 teaspoon smoked sweet paprika
4 garlic cloves, minced
1 minced shallot
4 bay leaves, crumbled
1 quart (4 cups) duck fat, melted

Rinse the duck legs and thighs and pat dry. Transfer to a 2-gallon resealable plastic bag.

Mix together the salt, sugar, coriander, cinnamon, paprika, garlic, shallot, and bay leaves. Coat the legs and thighs all over with the mixture. Close the bag and refrigerate for 24 to 48 hours, flipping it once a day.

Preheat the oven to 200°F.

Remove the legs and thighs from the bag, rinse thoroughly, and pat dry. Place in a 4-quart Dutch oven or other suitable pot and cover with the fat. Put the pot in the oven and cook for 8 to 10 hours. Remove from the oven and allow the duck to cool in the fat. Refrigerate in the fat until ready to use, at least 1 month.

Humility

Charcuterie is a craft that takes our most humble products and turns them into exquisite dishes. Clearly there is value in being humble—and lessons to be learned when you are not. When I was asked recently what the worst moment in my career has been, I didn't have to think long. When the broiler blew up in my face. That was the low point.

I wasn't even supposed to be cooking, just consulting. But when the restaurant's two cooks pulled a knife on me, I had to fire them. You can't really let that one slide. So, now, 1993, I was chef of this miserable little restaurant on Cleveland's West Side—a debt-ridden sinking ship with an owner who didn't know what she was doing, no cooks, and an exploded broiler—and I had no eyebrows.

I tried to shake my head clear to think. Six months earlier, I'd been a twenty-three-year-old rock star, executive chef at Piccolo Mondo, the hottest restaurant in town. What had happened? How had I ended up here?

A year and a half earlier, I had interviewed with a man named Carl Quagliata, Cleveland's legendary restaurateur. He had been preparing to open a new spot in the heart of the city and, after numerous interviews, he had hired me as sous chef. I'd been out of school two years and had worked only at Players, a thirty-eight-seat restaurant run by a self-trained chef-owner, where I'd quickly moved up to sous chef. Sous chef at Piccolo Mondo, a bigger, new restaurant, had looked like a good step up for me.

Shortly before we had opened, the executive chef had quit. I'd never been chef before and I had told Carl this. Carl had said I could do it. Now, Carl had a fire that drove him. He worked harder than any human I had ever met and demanded you do the same. He would yell at you, hug you, and kiss you all in the same breath. It was Carl who instilled in me that if you never let anyone outwork you, you will eventually succeed.

So we had opened and Piccolo Mondo, casual Italian food in a chic bistro setting, had quickly become one of the busiest, most successful restaurants the city had ever seen. We had been doing five hundred to six hundred covers a day and getting all kinds of media attention. I had been working a hundred hours a week—it was crazy. The line had been so busy that I once had sent out an osso bucco with no meat, just an empty bone on saffron risotto, to the corporate chef of Stouffer's, a big Cleveland food company. The guy had walked his plate into the kitchen and asked if it was some kind of joke. Not good.

But we had hired more staff, and Carl had brought in Doug Petkovic, a Chicago general manager who would become one of my friends and eventually a business partner, and we got things under control.

I'd been receiving so much praise from customers and the press, and the restaurant had been doing so well, that Carl had asked me if I would take over the kitchen of his flagship restaurant, Giovanni's, a high-end Italian place that had earned all kinds of awards from Distinguished Restaurants of North America (DiRoNA) and four diamonds from AAA and was one of the fanciest restaurants in the city, a culinary landmark. But Carl had felt it was stagnating. The clientele was an older generation, and he'd wanted to bring in a younger, hipper crowd. He'd wanted me to update some of the classics. With Piccolo Mondo the toast of the town and rocking on its own, I'd said, "No problem, Carl. Let me show you how it's done."

Problem was, no one had wanted to update the classics except me—not the kitchen, not the front-of-the-house staff, and not the customers. But that was too bad. I'd been brought in to do a job and I intended to do it. I'd been a rock star. I would simply work harder than anyone else. Here I had learned an important lesson about the power of staff. It's your family, and if they aren't with you, you aren't going anywhere. I had fought to change things, and they had fought back until it had gotten so hard that I didn't enjoy cooking anymore. I'd taken the Dover sole off the menu—an old-fashioned French dish that had had no place in a high-end Italian restaurant. Even though I'd taken it off the menu, the maître d' had continued to offer it as a special. As soon as we would run out of the sole, I'd figure that was it, but the maître d' had ordered and received it himself and would continue to offer it to his customers, cooking and serving it tableside!

I loved Carl, but I had had to get out of there. It was time to open a place of my own, and I had begun working on a restaurant deal. As soon as I had thought it was a sure thing, I had quit Giovanni's.

Only it wasn't a sure thing, and pretty soon I was digging up consulting work, pretty much always a low point in a chef's career—even when you're only twenty-three years old. You're brought into a failing restaurant to fix what usually can't be fixed—typically a lose-lose situation. On the West Side of Cleveland, a woman with some money who had always dreamed of owning a restaurant had opened up a little Italian place, hiring two cooks away from her favorite restaurant in Manhattan. The guys could put out OK food, but they knew the owner didn't know what she was doing, they were sloppy in the kitchen (smoking cigarettes on the line, for instance), and they'd begun to steal from her, so she had brought me in to save the restaurant. Suffice it to say that after I'd pushed the two New York goons a little too far, one of my few friends there, a waiter, had shouted my name and I had turned to see one of the cooks behind me and the other coming at me with a chef's knife.

That was when I went from consultant to head chef of a dying restaurant with no cooks.

I'd been chef of this restaurant for a few months when I heard through a friend that a new restaurant in the city was looking for a chef; this was my lifeline. The Caxton Café, forty seats and a tiny kitchen where I could do my own food. Business was slow, but it began to build from word of mouth. Within half a year we were doing enough business to increase the number of staff. I brought in the manager from my first restaurant, Liz Shanahan, and the dishwasher there who'd begun to cook, Frank Rogers. I called my friend Tim Bando, who'd been a manager at Piccolo. He'd come in early and wait tables at lunch and come back and work with me in the kitchen at night (Tim loves restaurants but hates people—so the kitchen is the perfect place for him!). These people would become my family, and are still family; Tim and Frank are as close to me as brothers, and Liz and I are married.

What I learned long ago at Giovanni's was, first, that hubris won't help you in a kitchen and second, that without the support of your staff, both back and front of the house, forget it. They are your family. From my next chef position on, my cooks and my waitstaff and my dishwashers all became family. Family had always guided me and it would continue to do so.

Pickles

If there's a single element of flavor that I think cooks need to focus on when they're working to improve their food, it's acidity. Controlling the level of acidity in your dishes is one of the most important skills you can develop; often a simple squeeze of lemon juice is all a dish needs to go from good to great. Acid may be second in importance only to salt as a seasoning device.

One of my favorite means of elevating one of my dishes is to add some form of pickle to it. Whereas Western culinary tradition demands a rich sauce to accompany a steak, for instance—a bordelaise or a béarnaise—I prefer to "sauce" the steak with a small salad of pickled chilies and olive oil. Though the flavor and richness of fat really satisfy, they can't truly be enjoyed unless they're balanced by acidity. Pickles deliver not only this acidity, but also sweetness (which balances the acidity) and the flavors of the pickled ingredient: the earthiness of turnip, the fruitiness and heat of chilies, for example. And last but not least, pickles add crunch.

Simply put: pickles are a lesson in what makes a dish work. They teach us about all the things that make one thing taste delicious and another just OK. Pickles teach us about fat and acid, sweetness and spiciness, and texture—five of the fundamental components of our food that we always need to pay attention to. Pickles are like a volume knob on your food.

Pickled vegetables have always been important in my restaurants. We began pickling so that we could buy ingredients at the peak of their season and preserve them to use all year. Ramps, one of my favorite vegetables, are a perfect example. Ramp season is very short, a few weeks or so in early spring, but they grow in abundance. When they do, we buy all we can get our hands on, up to a hundred pounds, and pickle them. Once they're pickled they're on hand to use on steaks, in salads, with rich braises, as a garnish for a charcuterie platter, in vinaigrettes along with some of the pickling liquid, or chopped and spread on a burger or a sausage.

So what began at Lola as a way to preserve the best food we could find became part of the defining style of our dishes. It's not only allowed us to deliver dynamic flavor, but also has enhanced and deepened our relationships with local farmers by making it possible to buy more of their produce during their growing season and use it throughout the year.

The four pickling techniques

Not all pickles are the same, and not all ingredients benefit from a single method. We use four different methods depending on the item being pickled and the end result we're after.
1. Vinegar brine over raw vegetables.
2. Warm vinegar brine over blanched vegetables.
3. Seasoned brine (no vinegar) over raw vegetables or meat.
4. Salt and seasonings (no liquid; also called a dry cure) over vegetables or raw meat.

The first technique is used for vegetables, such as red onions and tomatoes, that are naturally tender or that don't require cooking. The second technique is used for vegetables that need to be tenderized before being pickled, such as green beans and ramps. The third is used either to create a naturally fermented pickle, as with the traditional dill pickle, or to cure meat, such as beef and lamb's tongue. And in the fourth method, meat or vegetables are salted and the salt draws out water and creates its own brine; this is used for items such as salmon, pork belly, and cabbage, and it is sometimes referred to as a dry cure.

MASTER PICKLING RECIPE USING RED ONIONS

This is an excellent all-purpose pickling recipe that works for numerous vegetables. Because of both its simplicity and its versatility, it's a good starter recipe for those who haven't pickled before. Fennel pickled with this method is great with fish; I also love it with Lamb Sausage (page 105) with a dollop of Greek yogurt. Sliced garlic is amazing when pickled. Red onions are my most frequently used pickle both at home and in the restaurants, but any onion can be pickled this way. Use them on sandwiches and salads, on charcuterie plates, or to garnish a simply cooked piece of fish. Julienned or shaved celery, celery root, turnip, and carrot are all excellent choices here, too.

An exact amount of vinegar is not given here. The brine itself is half water, half vinegar, but because you can never know precisely how much of the water-vinegar mixture you'll need, I recommend fitting all the vegetables into the container you'll be using, filling it up with water, then dumping the water into a measuring cup, pouring out half, and replacing the half with vinegar.

Makes about 2 quarts

2 pounds red onions, sliced	1 tablespoon crushed red pepper flakes
White wine vinegar	2 tablespoons coriander seeds
Sugar	2 tablespoons black peppercorns
Kosher salt	4 garlic cloves
2 teaspoons mustard seeds	2 bay leaves

Pack the onions in two 1-quart jars and cover with water to come within ½ inch of the rim. Pour the water out into a measuring cup. Note the volume, pour off half the water, and replace it with vinegar. Add 2 tablespoons sugar and 2 tablespoons salt for every 3 cups of liquid.

Pour the vinegar mixture into a nonreactive saucepan, add the mustard seeds, red pepper flakes, coriander seeds, black peppercorns, garlic, and bay leaves, and bring to a boil over high heat. Allow the liquid to boil for 2 minutes, and then remove it from the heat.

Pour the hot liquid into the jars to cover the onions and screw on the lids. Refrigerate for up to 1 month.

PICKLED CHERRIES

These make a fantastic sweet-sour condiment that goes well with very rich dishes, everything from pork belly to foie gras, or even with some blue-veined cheese and crostini. But my favorite food to pair it with is duck; they were made for each other.

Makes about 2 quarts

2 pounds bing cherries
3 cups red wine vinegar
1½ cups sugar
2 tablespoons kosher salt
2 strips orange zest, removed with a
   vegetable peeler

1 teaspoon black peppercorns
2 cinnamon sticks
1 tablespoon coriander seeds
1 bay leaf

Prick each cherry with a fork several times and put them in a nonreactive jar or container.

Mix the vinegar, sugar, salt, orange zest, black peppercorns, cinnamon sticks, coriander seeds, and bay leaf in a nonreactive saucepan and bring to a boil. Reduce the heat so the liquid simmers, and cook for 10 minutes. Remove from the heat and let cool for 10 minutes.

Pour the liquid over the cherries (they should be completely submerged). When the concoction is completely cool, seal or cover the cherries, and refrigerate for up to 1 month.

PICKLED CHILIES

I love, love, love pickled chilies. Their natural heat is balanced by the sweetness and acid from the brine. Sliced, they are great strewn on grilled steaks or braised meats, and I also like to toss them with some parsley leaves, mint leaves, and olive oil for a little salad to garnish meats. The denser the flesh of the chile, the better luck you will have with the pickle; thin-skinned peppers such as poblanos and habaneros end up as mostly skin. In the summer in Cleveland many varieties of chilies abound, and pickling them allows me to load up for winter so that I can enjoy the sweet burn of summer throughout our often brutal winters.

My favorite chilies for pickling include fresno, jalapeño, Hungarian hot (banana pepper), and tomato pepper.

Makes about 2 quarts

2 pounds chilies	2 tablespoons coriander seeds
Sherry vinegar	2 tablespoons black peppercorns
Sugar	1 teaspoon cumin seeds
Kosher salt	4 sprigs of fresh marjoram
2 bay leaves	3 garlic cloves

Pack the chilies in two 1-quart jars and cover them with water to come within ½ inch of the rim. Pour the water out into a measuring cup. Note the volume, pour off half the water, and replace it with sherry vinegar. Add 2 tablespoons sugar and 2 table-spoons salt for every 3 cups of liquid.

Pour the vinegar mixture into a nonreactive saucepan and add the bay leaves, coriander seeds, black peppercorns, cumin seeds, marjoram, and garlic. Bring to a boil over high heat, then reduce the heat and simmer for 10 minutes. Remove from the heat and let cool slightly. Pour the hot liquid into the jars to cover the peppers, and screw on the lids. Refrigerate for up to 1 month.

PICKLED RAMPS

I always know it is officially spring when ramps start to pop up in my yard; these are the first things to grow. Ramps, also referred to as wild leeks, are indigenous to Ohio, West Virginia, Michigan, New York, and parts of Appalachia, too. They grow wild in the woods in damp areas in early spring for only about a month. A member of the lily family, they taste like a cross between leeks and garlic. When I get them I usually separate the leaves and the bulbs, saving the leaves to sauté in a little olive oil and use as a side dish for grilled meats and fish, or I chop them up to put in scrambled eggs. The bulbs I pickle so I can enjoy the ramps all year long. Pickled ramps are a great accompaniment to cured meats, are also excellent sliced in a salad, and can be used to top a variety of meats and fish.

Makes about 2 quarts

2 cups white wine vinegar
Kosher salt
2 teaspoons coriander seeds
1 teaspoon mustard seeds

1 bay leaf
1 jalapeño chile, split
2 pounds ramp bulbs (from 3 to 4 pounds ramps)

Combine the vinegar, 2 tablespoons salt, coriander seeds, mustard seeds, bay leaf, and jalapeño in a nonreactive saucepan and bring to a boil. Cook for 3 minutes. Remove the pan from the heat and let the liquid cool to room temperature.

Bring a gallon of heavily salted water to a boil. Blanch the ramps for 2 minutes in the boiling water and then drain in a colander.

Pack the ramps into two 1-quart jars, cover with the cooled pickling liquid to within ½ inch of the rim, and screw on the lids. Refrigerate for up to 1 month.

PICKLED GREEN TOMATOES

In the summertime in Cleveland we have a network of local farmers who supply our tomatoes. They always have a large quantity of green tomatoes that have fallen from the vine that they don't want to throw away. The green tomatoes are priced well, and we take as many as we can find because I love serving them pickled with rich grilled and braised meats.

Makes 2 quarts

3 fresno chilies, split
2 bay leaves
2 tablespoons coriander seeds
2 tablespoons cumin seeds
1 cinnamon stick
1 teaspoon cloves
1 teaspoon ground mace

2 tablespoons black peppercorns
5 garlic cloves
4 cups cider vinegar
¼ cup honey
2 tablespoons kosher salt
2 pounds green tomatoes of equal size

Combine the chilies, bay leaves, coriander seeds, cumin seeds, cinnamon stick, cloves, mace, black peppercorns, garlic, vinegar, honey, salt, and ½ cup water in a nonreactive saucepan and bring the liquid to a boil. Cook for 3 minutes. Remove the pan from the heat and let the liquid cool slightly.

Lightly prick each tomato 4 to 5 times with a wooden skewer. Place them in two 1-quart jars, cover them with the warm liquid, and screw on the lids. Refrigerate the tomatoes for up to 1 month.

PICKLED CUCUMBERS, GREEN BEANS, OR YELLOW WAX BEANS

This is a great table pickle. You'll often find it in pickle jars on deli counters to accompany sandwiches. But I like to put them in a tomato salad in place of regular cucumbers for a little twist, or I dice them up to add to a quick potato salad. The key to keeping the vegetable green is to blanch it first. The grape leaves are not just a nod to my Greek ancestry but also help in the fermentation process, as they're already fermented.

Makes about 2 quarts

Kosher salt
2 pounds small pickling cucumbers, green beans, yellow beans, or ¼-inch-thick slices of mature cucumbers
White wine vinegar
Sugar

7 garlic cloves, peeled
4 sprigs of fresh dill
2 fresno chilies
3 bay leaves
3 brined grape leaves

Bring a large pot of water to a boil and add enough salt so that it tastes like the ocean, about 1 cup per gallon. When the water returns to a boil, blanch the vegetables in the boiling water for 1 minute, then drain them, and run under cold water to cool.

Pack the vegetables in two 1-quart jars and cover them with water to come within ½ inch of the rim. Pour the water out into a measuring cup. Note the volume, pour off half the water, and replace it with vinegar. Add 2 tablespoons sugar and 2 tablespoons salt for every 3 cups of liquid.

Pour the vinegar mixture into a large bowl and add the garlic, dill, chilies, and bay leaves. Pour the liquid over the vegetables. Top with the grape leaves and weight down the ingredients with a ramekin or plate to ensure everything is submerged in brine.

Place the jars in a cool ventilated area for 1 to 2 weeks. The brine will become cloudy when the fermentation begins. When the liquid is clear, the fermentation is complete and you can seal the jars. The pickles are ready to eat immediately but will keep for up to 1 month in the refrigerator.

DILL PICKLES

I typically wouldn't defer to a writer for a good recipe, because they're usually so unreliable, but in a rare instance of writer trumps chef, Michael Ruhlman brought me some of these pickles one day, and I have to admit they are as good as any I have ever eaten. They're crunchy and salty, and they have that great natural acidity that develops during the fermentation process. The perfect pickle. Maybe Ruhlman is right: if you write about food long enough, you can actually learn how to cook! These are best with freshly picked young cucumbers, which are often available at farmers' markets.

Makes about 1 quart

3 tablespoons kosher salt
1 bunch of fresh dill

10 to 15 garlic cloves, to taste
1 pound pickling cucumbers

Combine 3¾ cups water with the salt, dill, and garlic in a saucepan and bring to a boil, stirring until the salt is dissolved. Remove the pan from the heat and let cool to room temperature.

Arrange the cucumbers in a nonreactive container, such as a 4-cup Pyrex measuring cup. Pour the brine over the cucumbers. Cover the cucumbers with plastic wrap and weight the cucumbers down with a small plate or bowl so that they're completely submerged. Set in a cool place and allow to ferment at room temperature for 1 week. Taste the cucumbers. If you want them to be more sour, leave them out for 2 more days.

To store them, strain the fermenting liquid into a nonreactive pan and bring to a boil, then remove it from the heat and allow to cool to room temperature. Pour the cooled brine back over the cucumbers, cover, and refrigerate for up to 1 month.

TURNIP KRAUT

Turnip kraut, which I pair with Poached Foie Gras Bratwurst (page 107), is excellent with any grilled sausage or roasted meat.

Makes about 1 quart

2½ pounds turnips, peeled and cut into
    long, thin matchsticks
1½ tablespoons kosher salt

½ teaspoon ground cumin
½ tablespoon coriander seeds

In a nonreactive container, toss the turnips with the salt and spices until they're evenly distributed. Weight the turnips down with a plate. They will release liquid. Press them down to ensure all the turnips are submerged. Discard any that isn't submerged. Store them in a cool dark place, optimally between 65°and 75°F. The liquid will begin to froth as fermentation takes hold. Allow them to ferment for four to eight weeks. When the frothing ends, the fermentation process is complete. Using a clean utensil, remove the turnips to a clean container or jar. Strain the liquid over the turnips, cover, and refrigerate until ready to use. This will keep for a month or more refrigerated.

PICKLED LAMB'S TONGUE

Pickled lamb's tongue is very mild, soft, and delicate. It's wonderful on a sandwich or as a garnish for a salad—two or three slices with mixed greens tossed with Sherry Vinaigrette (page 66), along with a toasted baguette, makes a great lunch or light meal—or it can be an intriguing garnish for a lean white fish, such as halibut with capers.

Don't be spooked by the tongues. If you like corned beef, you'll like pickled tongue—I guarantee it!

Serves 6

Cure
6 lamb's tongues
2 cups kosher salt
1 teaspoon pink salt (see page 97)
1 cup sugar

Grated zest of 1 lemon
2 garlic cloves, minced
1 cup fresh thyme leaves
1 tablespoon crushed red pepper flakes

Court bouillon
2 cups white wine
2 cups red wine vinegar
1 carrot, sliced

1 onion, sliced
2 garlic cloves
1 bay leaf

To cure the tongues, wash the tongues thoroughly and place them in a nonreactive container. Combine the kosher salt, pink salt, sugar, lemon zest, garlic, thyme, and red pepper flakes and coat the lamb's tongues with the mixture. Refrigerate, covered, for 6 days, turning the tongues once each day.

Rinse the cure off the tongues and place them in a 3-quart pot. Cover with the wine, vinegar, 2 cups water, carrot, onion, garlic, and bay leaf. Bring to a simmer, partially cover the pot, and keep the liquid at a gentle simmer for 2 hours. Take the pot off the heat and allow the tongues to cool in the liquid. Transfer the tongues and liquid to a nonreactive container, cover, and refrigerate until ready to use or for up to 1 month.

To serve the tongues, using a paring knife, peel the skin off each tongue and discard. Cut each tongue crosswise in ¼- to ⅜-inch-thick slices.

Stocks, Sauces, and Condiments

The biggest difference between cooking at home and cooking in the restaurants is that at the restaurants I have a nearly endless supply of ingredients and a large arsenal of prepared items on hand. Prepared stocks, dressings, and sauces make it a lot easier to put a dish together in a hurry. Here are the recipes that I always try to keep my home pantry stocked with. They all hold up very well and will help you avoid running out to the store to buy overly processed, overpriced junk. In the end they will save you not only time but also money.

Stocks

When I used to teach cooking classes and people asked if it was OK to substitute canned or boxed broth for homemade, I always said sure. Then I tasted the stuff. Most of it is terrible. It's so bad, in fact, that I'd prefer you use water instead.

I don't make a lot of intense reduction sauces; I find them gluey and feel that they mask the flavor of the dish rather than enhance it. I also tend to use pickles and acidic garnishes where others might use a rich stock. Nevertheless, stocks are the backbone of many soups, braises, and sauces. They're critical to so much of what we do at Lola and Lolita.

Stocks cook for a long time but they don't require a lot of work, and they freeze well. Allow stock to cool uncovered in your refrigerator after you strain it. Remove any fat that congeals on top. Cover and store for a week in your refrigerator or freeze in 2-cup portions for up to a month in your freezer. I use chicken stock for most of my cooking, whether making a quick sauce, cooking risotto, or braising pork belly.

You'll notice I use a lot of feet in my chicken stock because they're so rich in collagen, which melts into gelatin and gives the stock great body. This is a light white stock; for a richer, brown stock you can first roast the bones until golden brown, discard the fat, and follow the same method. The shellfish stock couldn't be more basic and really elevates all seafood dishes.

Finally, remember that if you're making a sauce that calls for stock and cooks for a long time (Yia Yia's Sunday Sauce, for instance, page 229), but you don't have fresh stock, a good trick is to add some water and bones to the long-simmering dish instead. Beef bones, veal bones, or even chicken bones can be added (though you'll want to remove them from the sauce; so you wouldn't want to add a lot of small chicken bones). Bones will provide much of the depth of flavor that adding fresh stock would have. Discard the bones before serving the dish.

CHICKEN STOCK

Makes about 3 quarts

2 pounds chicken backs and necks
2 pounds chicken feet, or additional
   backs and necks
1 onion, quartered
1 carrot, thickly sliced

1 head of garlic, halved crosswise
4 sprigs of fresh thyme
1 tablespoon kosher salt
1 bay leaf
1 tablespoon black peppercorns

Rinse the chicken parts thoroughly. In a 10-quart stockpot, combine the onion, carrot, garlic, thyme, salt, bay leaf, peppercorns, and 1 gallon cold water. Bring the liquid to a boil over high heat, skimming any foam and impurities that rise to the surface. Reduce the heat to low and simmer for 5 hours, skimming the surface as necessary. Strain through a fine-mesh strainer, discarding the solids.

SHELLFISH STOCK

Makes about 1 quart

Shells from 1 pound shrimp
1 onion, quartered
1 2-inch knob of peeled fresh ginger,
   sliced
1 carrot, thickly sliced

1 tablespoon coriander seeds, toasted
   (see Symon Says, page 69)
1 bay leaf
1 tablespoon kosher salt

Combine the shrimp shells, onion, ginger, carrot, coriander seeds, bay leaf, salt, and 2 quarts cold water in a pot. Bring the liquid to a boil over high heat, skimming away any impurities that rise to the surface. Reduce the heat to low and simmer for 2 hours, continuing to skim impurities as necessary. Strain through a fine-mesh strainer, discarding the solids.

SPICY KETCHUP

Heinz is tough to beat, but I like a ketchup with a little zing to it. This ketchup gets its kick from crushed red pepper and fresno chilies, and its depth of flavor from garlic, cumin, and cinnamon. It's a very versatile sauce, great on sandwiches or as a dipping sauce for fries; some people even order it at the restaurant to dip their steak in. And it's a great base for the Coffee Barbecue Sauce on page 135.

Makes 3 to 4 cups

1 small yellow onion, minced
3 garlic cloves, chopped
Kosher salt
1 tablespoon olive oil
5 fresno chilies, seeded and minced
1 ancho chile, seeded and minced
¼ teaspoon crushed red pepper flakes

2 tablespoons dark brown sugar
1 tablespoon cumin seeds
1 cinnamon stick
1 6-ounce can tomato paste
2 tablespoons cider vinegar

Sweat the onion and garlic with a three-finger pinch of salt in the olive oil over medium heat in a nonreactive 2-quart saucepan until translucent, about 2 minutes. Add the fresno chilies, ancho chile, and red pepper flakes. Cook for a minute or two. Add the brown sugar, cumin, cinnamon, tomato paste, and vinegar and simmer for 10 minutes. Add 3 cups water, bring to a gentle simmer, and cook over low heat for 2 hours.

Remove from the heat and let cool for 15 minutes. Discard the cinnamon stick. Purée the mixture in a blender and strain through a sieve, pushing any solids through. Let cool, then cover, and refrigerate for up to 1 month.

SYMON SAYS

Be careful when you purée hot liquids: Trapped hot air will shoot the lid off your blender when you start it up. It's best to remove the center piece of the lid and cover the opening with a kitchen towel, holding it down over the lid when you start the blender, to prevent a scalding mess.

LOLA STEAK SAUCE

Over time, I simply got tired of saying no when people asked me for steak sauce; God bless Cleveland, but it's a little too reliant on A1. This is a delicious balsamic-based sauce that's sweet, acidic, and spicy from the cloves and cumin and picks up some depth from the anchovy. It's a great sauce for simply grilled steaks or game, and it's delicious on a burger.

Makes 1 cup

2 cups balsamic vinegar
2 tablespoons red wine vinegar
½ cup raisins
1 small yellow onion, diced (½ cup)
3 garlic cloves
2 tablespoons dark brown sugar

½ teaspoon whole cloves
½ teaspoon cumin seeds
½ tablespoon celery salt
1 sprig of fresh rosemary
1 or 2 salt-packed anchovy fillets, rinsed
   and chopped (1 tablespoon)

Combine the balsamic and red wine vinegars, raisins, onion, garlic, brown sugar, cloves, cumin, celery salt, rosemary, and anchovies in a large nonreactive saucepan and cook over medium-low heat until the mixture has reduced by one third. Pour through a fine-mesh strainer twice or until you have a nice smooth sauce; discard the solids. Let cool, then cover, and refrigerate in a jar for up to 1 month.

COFFEE BARBECUE SAUCE

This sauce has great complexity and depth of flavor—or guts, as I call it. Bitterness and acidity come from the coffee, acidity from the sherry vinegar, spice from the coriander, spicy heat from the chipotle powder; and its backbone is provided by homemade ketchup. It's a great all-around sauce for poultry, grilled beef, and pork.

We also make a version of this without the sugar and with twice the vinegar, which I prefer with fattier cuts and smoked meats.

Makes 3 cups

1 small yellow onion, minced
1 tablespoon olive oil
Kosher salt
1½ tablespoons coriander seeds, toasted
  (see Symon Says, page 69)
½ cup packed dark brown sugar

½ cup sherry vinegar
1 cup strong coffee
1 cup Spicy Ketchup (page 133)
½ cup tomato juice
½ tablespoon chipotle powder

Sweat the onion in the olive oil with a good pinch of salt in a nonreactive 2-quart saucepan over medium-low heat until translucent, about 2 minutes. Add the coriander, brown sugar, vinegar, and coffee and simmer for 10 minutes. Add the ketchup, tomato juice, and chipotle powder, and simmer for 2 hours. Strain, discard the solids, and let cool. Store covered in the refrigerator for up to 1 month.

RED PEPPER RELISH

I love to have this in my fridge all the time. Sweet, tangy, spicy, and citrusy, it livens up eggs and sandwiches and makes a brightly flavored sauce for grilled fish.

Makes 2 cups

1 tablespoon olive oil
½ small red onion, finely diced
2 garlic cloves, minced
Kosher salt
2 red bell peppers, cored, seeded, and
   finely diced
2 jalapeños, seeded and diced

1 tablespoon coriander seeds, toasted
   (see Symon Says, page 69)
¼ cup packed dark brown sugar
¼ cup white wine vinegar
½ cup fresh orange juice
½ cup chopped fresh cilantro

Heat a medium nonreactive saucepan over medium-low heat. Add the olive oil to glaze the bottom of the pan. Add the onion, garlic, and a pinch of salt and sweat until the onion begins to soften, about 2 minutes. Add the bell peppers and jalapeños and sweat for 2 more minutes. Add the coriander seeds and cook for another 30 seconds.

Add the sugar and vinegar and cook, stirring, until the sugar dissolves. Add the orange juice and simmer, stirring occasionally, until the liquid completely reduces, about 10 minutes. Remove from the heat and allow the relish to cool to room temperature. Season with salt to taste and fold in the cilantro. Refrigerate for up to 1 month.

SHASHA SAUCE

This is a verbatim family recipe, made every year with the abundant banana peppers Liz's mom grows. Look at the ingredients and you'll see how weird this is; no chef would come up with such a thing, especially yellow mustard and the funky flour paste that's added at the end. But I'm telling you it's fantastic; the whole family is addicted to this stuff. I love it with scrambled eggs, on cold cuts, with Roasted Rack of Pork (page 242), as seasoning for a vinaigrette, and as a dipping sauce for Pig's Ears (see page 38). If Sherla has a bad year and doesn't get enough peppers and I don't get a couple jars, I get depressed. And I get depressed when I run out of this stuff.

Makes about 3 cups

12 hot banana peppers
4 garlic cloves
1 cup yellow mustard

1 cup white wine vinegar
¾ cup sugar
⅓ cup all-purpose flour

Slice off the top of the peppers and coarsely chop them. Toss them into a food processor with the garlic, mustard, and vinegar, and purée.

Pour the purée into a nonreactive saucepan, add the sugar, and bring to a boil over high heat. Lower the heat and simmer for 30 minutes.

Mix the flour and ½ cup water to a smooth paste. Whisk it into the simmering liquid and return the mixture to a simmer. Cook for 20 to 30 minutes, stirring regularly, until very thick. Let the sauce cool, pour it into a nonreactive container, and refrigerate for up to 1 month.

HORSERADISH CRÈME FRAÎCHE

This sauce uses the natural bacteria in the buttermilk to generate acid, resulting in a cultured cream we call crème fraîche—cream with a subtle natural sourness. Yes, you could use store-bought crème fraîche, but that takes some of the fun out of the recipe. We serve this piquant horseradish sauce with Beef Cheek Pierogies (page 45), but it goes well with all roasted or braised beef and is great on a sandwich.

Makes 1¼ cups

1 cup heavy cream
1 tablespoon buttermilk
¼ cup grated fresh horseradish

1 tablespoon chopped fresh chives
1 teaspoon coarsely ground black pepper
Kosher salt

Heat the heavy cream in a small saucepan over low heat to 105°F. Remove from the heat and whisk in the buttermilk. Cover the pan with plastic wrap and leave in a warm place (90° to 100°F is optimal; the cooler the temperature the longer fermentation may take) for 36 to 48 hours.

When the cream has thickened, chill it in the refrigerator for a few hours, until cold, or for up to 1 week. Before serving, fold in the horseradish, chives, pepper, and salt to taste.

AIOLI

This is a straightforward aioli, a garlicky fresh mayonnaise made with olive oil. It can be taken in any number of directions and can be seasoned with chopped fresh herbs or powerful flavors such as anchovy (see page 148). I recommend you use farm-fresh eggs or organic eggs for raw yolk preparations such as this one. And remember that since this sauce is primarily olive oil, the better the quality of the oil you use, the better your aioli will taste.

Makes ¼ cup

1 large egg yolk
3 garlic cloves, smashed with the flat side
    of a knife and minced to a paste

2 to 3 teaspoons lemon juice, to taste
¼ teaspoon kosher salt
1 cup extra-virgin olive oil

Whisk the egg yolk, garlic, lemon juice, and salt in a bowl. While whisking continuously, begin adding the oil drop by drop until an emulsion is achieved. Continue adding the oil in a thin stream until all the oil is incorporated. The sauce will keep, covered and refrigerated, for up to a week.

TZATZIKI SAUCE

This is a classic Greek sauce that goes well with all lamb dishes. It's the traditional sauce for gyros and makes a great dipping sauce for fritters and keftedes (see page 11).

Makes about 4 cups

2 cups Greek yogurt
1 cucumber
Kosher salt
Juice of 2 lemons

3 tablespoons chopped fresh mint
1 tablespoon minced garlic
1 tablespoon minced shallot
Freshly ground black pepper

Put the yogurt in a cheesecloth-lined strainer set over a bowl and let drain for 24 hours in the refrigerator. Peel and dice the cucumber. Sprinkle it with salt and place in a strainer at room temperature for 2 to 3 hours to drain.

Stir together the yogurt, cucumber, lemon juice, mint, garlic, and shallot in a medium bowl until thoroughly combined. Season to taste with salt and pepper.

Side Dishes

Sides take a meal over the top. The main course, a big roast or a grilled meat, can be—should usually be—simple and straightforward, and when it's combined with a couple of great sides, the whole meal gets better. So try every now and then to think of the sides first: Pick one or two that you think work well together and then choose a main course.

Like soups, they're very seasonal. Let the ingredients at your local market inspire you. Buy what's fresh and in season, and let that guide your choice of side dishes.

These are some of my favorite sides that I serve at the restaurant and at home. They're great as they are but they're even better combined. Side dishes are fun, and the more fun you have with them, the better the whole meal will be.

OHIO CREAMED CORN WITH BACON

Ohio sweet corn is the best in the world and I like to feature it in a dish that to me is about childhood comforts. This has great flavors not only from the corn, but also from bacon and, importantly, from a stock I make from the cobs. Cobs release a lot of sweetness from the corn that remains attached after the kernels are cut—flavor that's an important part of the dish. I also add onion, garlic, coriander, and a bay leaf to the stock, which I then use to cook the corn and bacon. The stock is reduced, then thickened and enriched with crème fraîche and finished with lime zest. I can't think of a dish that this doesn't go with—pork, chicken, beef, fish, grilled, roasted, or sautéed—but my favorite match is sautéed scallops.

Serves 4 to 6

5 ears of corn
1 teaspoon extra-virgin olive oil
¼ pound thick-cut bacon, cut into 1-inch
    strips
1 medium yellow onion, diced
1 garlic clove, minced

1 teaspoon kosher salt, or more to taste
½ recipe Corn Cob Stock (page 53)
½ cup crème fraîche
1 tablespoon unsalted butter
½ cup chopped fresh cilantro
Grated zest of 1 lime

Cut the kernels from the cobs and set the kernels aside. (Use the cobs to make the stock.)

Heat a large saucepan over medium heat and glaze the bottom with the olive oil. Add the bacon and cook, stirring as needed, to render the fat and brown the pieces, 5 minutes. Add the onion and sweat it for about 45 seconds. Add the garlic and continue to cook, stirring, for another 30 seconds. Add the reserved corn and the salt and cook for 2 minutes.

Pour in the corn cob stock and bring to a simmer. Cook until the liquid reduces to approximately 1 cup, 10 minutes. Add the crème fraîche and simmer until the mixture begins to thicken, about 3 minutes. Stir in the butter. Remove the pan from the heat and stir in the cilantro and lime zest. Season with salt if needed before serving.

PEAS AND PANCETTA

I make this dish when peas are at the height of their season and I love to serve it with simply cooked fish such as grilled halibut or grilled salmon. It needs some acidity because of the richness of the pancetta and rendered fat. Since I don't love lemon and bacon together, I opt for orange juice and zest; the brightness they add works perfectly here.

Serves 4

¼ pound pancetta, diced (1 cup)
1 shallot, sliced
1 teaspoon minced garlic
Grated zest and juice of 1 orange

1 cup shelled fresh peas
¼ cup sliced fresh flat-leaf parsley leaves
1 tablespoon unsalted butter
Kosher salt

Cook the pancetta in a large sauté pan over medium-low heat until the fat is rendered and the pancetta is crispy, about 5 minutes. Add the shallot and garlic, sweat for 1 minute, and then add the orange juice.

Increase the heat to medium, add the peas, and cook until they're tender, about 2 minutes. Remove the pan from the heat and fold in the orange zest, parsley, and butter. Taste for seasoning and add salt if necessary, though you shouldn't need much if any because the pancetta adds a natural saltiness to the dish.

CRISPY CAULIFLOWER WITH ANCHOVY AIOLI

Cauliflower is an underrated, underused vegetable. Roasted, sautéed, fried, it's delicious and satisfying and it can almost always replace potatoes if you're looking to reduce your starchy carbs. But you shouldn't need any justification; just start using it more. I love preparing it tempura style—it's got an almost creamy consistency here—and serving it with an anchovy aioli. To ratchet up the flavor even more, I blanch the cauliflower first in a spicy court bouillon, though the cauliflower can also be battered and fried raw.

Serves 4

1 red onion, quartered
1 head of garlic, split through its equator
1 tablespoon crushed red pepper flakes
1 tablespoon coriander seeds, toasted
  (page 69)
Kosher salt
2 lemons
1 head of cauliflower, cut into large
  florets

Canola oil, for deep-frying
Aioli (page 141)
4 salt-packed anchovies, rinsed, filleted,
  and minced
1 tablespoon sliced fresh flat-leaf parsley
  leaves
Tempura Batter (recipe follows)

Combine the onion, garlic, red pepper flakes, coriander, a large pinch of salt, and 1 quart water in a 4-quart pot. Quarter one of the lemons and add it to the pot. Bring the liquid to a boil, reduce the heat, and simmer for 30 minutes. Strain the liquid, return it to the pot, and bring it back to a boil.

Fill a medium bowl halfway with ice water.

Blanch the cauliflower florets for 1 minute in the boiling liquid. Drain and transfer to the ice water until chilled. Drain the cauliflower thoroughly and set aside on paper towels.

Pour enough oil into a medium pot so that the oil comes 3 inches up the sides. Heat the oil to 350°F.

While the oil is heating, make the sauce. Grate the zest from the remaining lemon and squeeze its juice. In a small bowl, stir together the zest, juice, aioli, anchovies, and parsley.

Lightly coat the cauliflower in the tempura batter and fry, turning once, until golden brown, about 4 minutes. Remove with a slotted spoon and drain on paper towels.

Serve the crispy cauliflower with the sauce for dipping.

TEMPURA BATTER

I love fried food, and this tempura batter is great to use on anything that you want to fry, including vegetables or shrimp or other seafood. Traditionally tempura batter includes egg, but I like a very light and crisp batter made from nothing more than rice flour (available in Middle Eastern and Indian markets), seltzer water, and seasoning. This batter gets very crisp and will give whatever you are frying a terrific crunch.

Makes 1½ cups

⅔ cup cake flour, plus ½ cup for dusting
⅓ cup cornstarch
1 teaspoon kosher salt
1½ teaspoons coriander seeds, toasted
    (see Symon Says, page 69) and
    ground

1 teaspoon smoked paprika
¼ teaspoon cayenne pepper
About 1 cup sparkling water

Combine the flour, cornstarch, salt, coriander, paprika, and cayenne in a mixing bowl. When you're ready to fry, stir in enough sparkling water to make a light batter that has the consistency of heavy cream.

Important But Under-Recognized Tools

What do I need in the kitchen? One knife—a chef's knife, that's it; a cutting board; a big rondeau (a wide flat round pot with shallow sides; I could cook just about anything in one, or invert it for a griddle); I'd need a flat-edged wooden spoon, a whisk, a fine-mesh sieve for straining, and an off-set slotted spatula, usually called a fish spatula (or Peltex). I could cook forever with these few tools; they're common to all chefs more or less. But there are a few other tools that I couldn't do without and because they're a little more idiosyncratic, I think they are meaningful to discuss.

Microplane

The Microplane grater changed my life. It altered forever the finishing of my dishes. Suddenly citrus zest became available *à la minute*. In a restaurant situation, on the line, I've got a lot of plates going out. I'm not going to have a box grater taking up space on my station during a busy service. I'm not going to be slicing the skin off a lemon, removing the pith, and chopping it during service. One, I don't have time, and two, in that process the lemon loses all the oils that make it such an amazing seasoning. But the Microplane, a slender handheld rasp that slices off just the zest at just the right depth so you don't get any of the pith, changed my seasoning strategy. Suddenly I began using tons of zest and realized what a transformative ingredient it is. With its volatile oils and flavor, citrus zest is one of the most powerful seasonings there is—it's more flavorful than the juice—and one of the most underutilized, especially in the home kitchen. What doesn't taste better with some lemon zest on it? Fish, meat, pasta, braised meats, shellfish, salads—even ice cream and sweets. And then there's orange and lime and grapefruit zest. These are common fruits from which we too often take the fruit and throw away the best part.

A Microplane is also the perfect tool for grating and shaving many foods. I use it to grate cinnamon and nutmeg over savory food (cinnamon is amazing with shellfish and gives extraordinary depth to braised meats), as well as to grate or shave Parmesan cheese and chocolate. They're available with different size grates—I prefer a fine one for zest and a coarse one for cheese.

Bench Scraper

When I don't have a bench scraper it's like not being able to find a pen when I need it—I simply always have one around. This four-by-six-inch piece of plastic, which costs a buck or two, is a simple utilitarian device that makes every job easier and cleaner. I use it to move food from one place to another, which I do all day long when I'm cooking: diced onion into a hot pan, scraps into the bin. Please don't ever drag the sharp edge of your knife over your board to do this! The plastic bench scraper is an appendage. I use it to mix things and my hands stay dry, which is more efficient. It cuts dough and separates food. For the home cook and for the restaurant cook alike, the bench scraper helps you work cleaner and more efficiently.

Peppermill for Spices

Spices make a huge difference in food, and I use them everywhere. They're one of the secrets to flavors that pop; they make food complex and intriguing. Spices are best purchased whole and cracked, crushed, chopped, ground, or pulverized as needed. They should almost always be toasted before being ground because that doubles or triples their flavor. Thanks to Derek Clayton, Lola's chef de cuisine, I use a Peugeot peppermill for my spices, the BMW of grinders. It's not crazy expensive but it's solid—and it performs perfectly. You need a grinder that grinds fine enough; so that the seasoning is evenly distributed and won't get stuck between your teeth.

Food Mill

A stainless-steel food mill should be a part of every home kitchen. At the restaurants we have all kinds of devices to pulverize or blend food and strain food, but the food mill is an all-purpose device that does many tasks, from puréeing to straining. Potatoes are easily riced and don't become gluey when passed through a food mill. Tomatoes turn immediately into sauce, the seeds strained out. Puréed soups are a breeze. When you're finished, just put the food mill parts in the dishwasher for easy cleanup.

BRAISED ENDIVE WITH CITRUS

I love the natural bitterness of endive. Here I brown it first so it develops some sweetness and then braise it in orange juice and stock, which adds to the sweetness. The endive should be cooked all the way through, but it should still have some bite to it; it should not be mushy. This is a great side for rich or fatty foods, such as duck, a rib-eye steak, or even braised dishes like veal shank or short ribs.

Serves 4

2 tablespoons olive oil
4 Belgian endives, halved lengthwise
Kosher salt
2 garlic cloves, sliced
6 sprigs of fresh thyme

Grated zest and juice of 1 orange
½ cup Chicken Stock (page 131)
2 tablespoons honey
4 tablespoons (½ stick) unsalted butter

Preheat the oven to 325°F.

Heat a large ovenproof sauté pan over medium heat and add the olive oil. Place the endive in the pan, cut side down, season with salt, and cook until nicely browned, about 5 minutes. Add the garlic and sweat it for 1 minute. Add the thyme, orange zest and juice, stock, and honey. Bring to a simmer and then place the pan in the oven until the endive is cooked through and tender, about 20 minutes.

Remove the endive from the pan to a platter. Reduce the pan liquid over high heat to about ⅓ cup, swirl in the butter, and spoon the liquid over the endive.

BRAISED GREENS WITH SMOKY BACON

Liz's mom makes collards, but I love any hardy green—chard, kale, mustard greens, beet greens—that can stand up to an hour's cooking time in their own juices and take on the big flavors of bacon, garlic, and chilies. I finish them with a little honey and, depending how hot the chilies are, a shot of Tabasco or Sriracha sauce. This is what winter vegetables are all about.

Serves 4

½ pound slab bacon
3 tablespoons duck fat, lard, or olive oil
2 garlic cloves, sliced
2 shallots, sliced
2 fresno chilies, seeded and sliced
1 pound hearty braising greens, tough
    stems removed

¼ cup sherry vinegar
Kosher salt
¼ cup wildflower honey
Tabasco sauce

In a 6-quart saucepan over medium heat, cook the piece of bacon in the fat until the bacon begins to render some of its own fat, about 5 minutes. Add the garlic, shallots, and chilies and sweat them for about 2 minutes. Add the greens and reduce the heat to low. Add the vinegar, a large pinch of salt, and the honey. Simmer the greens until they're tender, about 1 hour. Season to taste with salt and Tabasco sauce.

FRIED BRUSSELS SPROUTS WITH WALNUTS AND CAPERS

I love Brussels sprouts and I cook them many ways—boiled, roasted, sautéed—but deep-frying them is the best. They develop a great flavor and a texture that you can't get any other way. These are served with walnuts and a sharp red wine vinaigrette seasoned with anchovies and garlic. It's an excellent side dish in fall and winter, and it goes especially well with big roasted meats. You can also take this in an Asian direction by omitting the capers and anchovies and adding soy sauce, fish sauce, grated ginger, and sriracha sauce.

Serves 6 to 8

Canola oil, for deep-frying

1 garlic clove, minced

4 salt-packed anchovy fillets, rinsed, filleted, and minced

1 serrano chile, seeded and minced

¼ cup red wine vinegar

1 tablespoon honey

2 scallions, white and green parts, thinly sliced on the bias

½ cup walnut pieces, toasted (see Symon Says, page 69) and coarsely chopped

½ cup extra-virgin olive oil

1 pound Brussels sprouts, trimmed and quartered lengthwise

2 cups loosely packed fresh flat-leaf parsley leaves

2 tablespoons salt-packed capers, rinsed and patted dry

Kosher salt and freshly ground black pepper

Pour enough oil into a medium pot so that the oil comes 3 inches up the sides. Heat the oil to 350°F.

While the oil is heating, whisk together the garlic, anchovies, serrano, red wine vinegar, honey, scallions, walnuts, and extra-virgin olive oil in a bowl large enough to toss all the Brussels sprouts. Keep the bowl near the stovetop.

Working in batches, deep-fry the Brussels sprouts until the edges begin to curl and brown, about 3 minutes. To the last batch, add the parsley and capers (stand back—the capers will pop and sputter!). Give the contents of the pot a stir. When the color of the parsley becomes a deeper, more saturated shade of green, about ½ to 1 minute, remove the contents of the pot with a skimmer and place directly into the bowl of dressing. Toss to coat. Add salt and pepper to taste.

CHICKPEAS AND SKORDALIA

There are two different skordalia sauces in Greece. One is made with potatoes and garlic, puréed until smooth, and the other with day-old bread, almonds, and garlic, puréed with lemon and olive oil so that it has a consistency like hummus. This is the one I really like. Traditionally, it's served under fried fish, but it also makes a nice spread. Here chickpeas are folded into the skordalia to give it a great texture. This would be perfect with roast chicken (see page 238; omit the salsa) or hanger steak (see page 204). It can be made a couple of days ahead and refrigerated.

Serves 6 to 8

2 cups ½-inch cubed crustless day-old
 bread
1 cup whole milk
4 garlic cloves
Grated zest and juice of 1 lemon
1 cup almonds, toasted (see page 69)

¾ cup extra-virgin olive oil
Kosher salt
1 cup cooked chickpeas
3 tablespoons chopped fresh flat-leaf
 parsley leaves

Cover the bread with the milk and let it soak for 30 minutes.

Using your hands, wring excess milk from the bread (reserve the milk) and put the bread in a blender with the garlic, lemon juice, almonds, olive oil, and a three-finger pinch of salt. Purée this mixture until smooth, adding some of the reserved milk to bring it to a thick, hummus-like consistency. Transfer to a bowl and stir in the chickpeas. Taste for seasoning, adding more salt if needed. Stir in the parsley and lemon zest before serving.

GRILLED RADICCHIO WITH ORANGE AND BALSAMIC

This side is super easy and fast. It can be cooked on a grill or in a grill pan in less than five minutes. It's a great side dish in spring and summer when you're also grilling lamb chops or steaks. The grilling takes out some of the bitterness and brings out the lettuce's sweetness, as do the orange and balsamic. You could also add a drizzle of honey and a sprinkle of chopped rosemary to this for a little more complexity, but it's refreshing just with the vinegar and OJ.

Serves 4 to 6

2 heads of radicchio, quartered through the core
1 tablespoon olive oil
Kosher salt and freshly ground black pepper

1 tablespoon extra-virgin olive oil
1 tablespoon balsamic vinegar
Grated zest and juice of 1 orange

Preheat the grill.

Drizzle the radicchio with the olive oil and sprinkle with salt and pepper.

Grill the radicchio for 2 minutes per side on a hot grill. Remove to a serving platter; sprinkle with salt and pepper; drizzle with the extra-virgin olive oil, balsamic, orange juice, and orange zest; and serve.

SEARED WILD MUSHROOMS

The biggest mistake people make in cooking mushrooms is not getting their pan and oil hot enough before they add the mushrooms. When the pan and oil are too cool, the mushrooms begin releasing their water into the pan, which prevents them from getting a good sear—the source of so much flavor. Another mistake is crowding the pan with too many mushrooms, which also results in steamed mushrooms. So cook your mushrooms in batches if necessary, and if you're using a variety, cook only the same kind together, because they cook at different rates. I add garlic and shallots at the end of the cooking so that they don't burn.

Seared and sautéed mushrooms go well with most meats and hearty fish, such as salmon or halibut.

Serves 4 to 6

1 pound wild mushrooms, preferably a mixture of oyster, chanterelle, and lobster
Olive oil or canola oil, for sautéing
Kosher salt

Small bunch of fresh thyme
2 shallots, thinly sliced
2 garlic cloves, thinly sliced
1 teaspoon unsalted butter

Slice the oyster mushrooms ¼ inch thick. Quarter or halve chanterelles lengthwise to make pieces of a similar size. Slice lobster mushrooms ⅛ inch thick.

Heat a large sauté pan over medium-high heat for 20 to 30 seconds. Glaze the bottom of the pan with oil. Lay in the oyster mushrooms, taking care not to crowd the pan. Sprinkle the mushrooms with salt and add a few sprigs of thyme. Sauté, turning the mushrooms to brown them on both sides, about 6 minutes. Remove the mushrooms from the pan and set aside on a plate. Check the pan to see if you need to add another glaze of oil. Repeat the sautéing of the mushrooms, cooking each variety independently, and seasoning each batch with salt and sprigs of thyme.

When you are finished sautéing all of the mushrooms, add another glaze of oil to the pan if needed, and add the shallots and a sprinkle of salt. Cook for 30 seconds, then add the garlic, and cook for another 30 seconds. Add all of the mushrooms and the butter, stirring. When the butter has melted, the mushrooms are ready to serve.

SOFT POLENTA WITH MASCARPONE

The first step in making great polenta is buying great polenta. Chef Jan Birnbaum turned me on to Anson Mills, in South Carolina, eight or nine years ago, and I've never used any other company's cornmeal since. Their milled organic heirloom grains are simply the best. The company also sells excellent grits and flours (see Sources, page 250).

Creamy polenta is like Italian mashed potatoes. Anytime you want a change from mashed potatoes, polenta makes a perfect substitute. In fact, I like to cook polenta to mashed-potato consistency—soft enough that it relaxes a little when it hits the plate, not too stiff, not too loose. Any leftovers can be refrigerated. Once the mixture sets up and becomes firm, it can be cut and fried or even grilled.

Serves 6 to 8

6 tablespoons (¾ stick) unsalted butter
½ small yellow onion, minced (½ cup)
1 garlic clove, minced
4 cups Chicken Stock (page 131)

2 cups Anson Mills polenta
¼ cup mascarpone
¼ cup grated Parmesan cheese
Kosher salt

In a 4-quart saucepan, melt 2 tablespoons of the butter over medium heat. Add the onion and garlic and sweat them until translucent and aromatic, 5 minutes. Add the stock and bring to a simmer. Slowly add the polenta while whisking and reduce the heat to low. Cook over low heat for 2 hours, stirring frequently. Remove from the heat and whisk in the mascarpone, Parmesan, and remaining 4 tablespoons butter. Season to taste with salt.

WHIPPED ROOT VEGETABLES

This is a delicious substitute for mashed potatoes. The celery root and parsnips give the whipped vegetables a nice sweetness, while the turnips add a touch of contrasting bitterness. You still get the satisfying richness of mashed potatoes but you'll keep your guests guessing as to what's in them and why they taste so unusual and good. I prefer to use a food mill to "mash" the potatoes, but you can use a hand masher as well.

Serves 8 to 10

½ pound potatoes (about 1 large russet)
½ pound parsnips (about 2 medium)
½ pound celery root (about 1 medium)
¼ pound turnips (about 2 medium)

2 tablespoons kosher salt, plus more to taste
½ pound (2 sticks) unsalted butter, cut into small pieces

Peel the potatoes, parsnips, celery root, and turnips and cut into 1- to 2-inch pieces. Combine them in a large pot and cover with twice the volume of cold water and 1 tablespoon of the salt. Bring the water to a boil over high heat, reduce the heat to medium, and boil gently until the vegetables are tender (insert a paring knife into a potato; there will be no resistance when they're cooked), 20 to 30 minutes.

Strain the vegetables well and return to the pot. Let the pot sit for 5 minutes over low heat to cook off any excess liquid. Run the hot vegetables through a food mill into a large bowl. Add the remaining tablespoon salt and then whip in the butter.

SYMON SAYS

Make sure your mix of vegetables is relatively dry after they are cooked and strained or they may be runny. The other big key here is to make sure your water is salted correctly when boiling the mix. Taste it; the water should taste pleasantly seasoned.

RED POTATOES WITH ARUGULA

This dish of potatoes seasoned with mustard and spicy arugula and enriched with cream is an excellent, easy way to enliven basic potatoes and goes well with most meats and fish. I made this originally as a bed for the Mushroom-Stuffed Brick-Roasted Chicken on page 198.

Serves 4 to 6

2 pounds 2-inch red potatoes
Kosher salt
½ cup heavy cream
½ cup Chicken Stock (page 131)

2 tablespoons whole-grain Dijon mustard
2 tablespoons unsalted butter
Freshly ground black pepper
¼ to ½ pound arugula

Put the potatoes in a large pot and add enough water to cover by 2 inches. Season the water well with salt and bring to a boil. Cook until the potatoes are tender when pierced with a knife, 30 to 40 minutes. Drain them and let the moisture steam off. When they're cool enough to handle, peel them if you wish. Cut into ½-inch-thick slices.

In a medium sauté pan, whisk together the cream, stock, and mustard. Reduce by one-third over high heat, about 5 minutes. Add the potatoes and toss to coat. Stir in the butter and season with salt and pepper to taste. When the cream comes to a simmer, add the arugula. Continue to cook until the arugula is completely wilted, about 45 seconds.

DAD'S POTATO PANCAKES

My dad worked the midnight shift at a Ford Motors plant throughout most of my childhood, so when he got home, we were just getting up. He used to make us meals that worked as both our breakfast and his dinner, hearty sandwiches with eggs on top and these potato pancakes. To us, he was the king of breakfast. I don't think my sister, Nikki, loved anything more than his potato pancakes. They're the best I know, light, thin, and crisp. Now that I've worked my share of late nights, I realize how hard starting his shift at midnight must have been for him, both physically and emotionally. When his shift was done, he could have hit the drive-through and picked up fast food, but he didn't. I'm sure he missed us and so he'd come home and cook for us. All the men in my family cooked. Those breakfasts he made are some of my best childhood memories and serve now to remind me what a powerful force food is in bringing people together.

I always had these for breakfast as a kid, but they make a great side dish for roasted chicken, grilled steak, just about any meat. In the summer I add some grated zucchini for another layer of flavor.

Serves 8

4 medium russet potatoes (about 2 pounds)
1 large egg, beaten
¼ teaspoon baking powder
1 tablespoon all-purpose flour
1 teaspoon kosher salt
¼ teaspoon freshly ground black pepper
1 medium yellow onion
8 tablespoons (1 stick) unsalted butter

Preheat the oven to 200°F.

Peel the potatoes and keep them submerged in cold water. In a mixing bowl, whisk together the egg, baking powder, flour, salt, and pepper. Using the large holes on a box grater, grate the onion and add it to the egg mixture. Grate the potatoes onto a clean kitchen towel and wring as much water out of them as you can. Add the potatoes to the egg mixture. Toss so that the mixture is evenly combined.

Heat a medium sauté pan over medium heat and melt half of the butter in it. Using half of the potato mixture, shape 4 pancakes, each about 4 inches in diameter and about ½ inch thick. Sauté the pancakes in the butter until each side is golden brown and the interior is cooked through, 15 to 20 minutes. Transfer them to a plate lined with paper towels and keep them warm in the oven while you shape and cook 4 more pancakes using the remaining butter and potato mixture.

CRAB TATER TOTS

These are simply potato croquettes—*pâte à choux* mixed with mashed potatoes—loaded with crab meat. Customers at Lola kept asking me to get crab on the menu, but I didn't want to do crab cakes like every other restaurant; I wanted to do something different. Tater tots would be something my customers would be familiar with and they'd provide that same satisfaction—the Cleveland version of the crab cake. These add texture and flavor to grouper (see page 175), but they also make a great side dish or even an appetizer, served with some Red Pepper Relish (page 136) and Shasha Sauce (page 138).

The tater tots can be prepared up to a day before you intend to cook and serve them. The croquette mixture is a great way to make use of leftover mashed potatoes.

Serves 6 to 8

2 tablespoons unsalted butter
¼ cup all-purpose flour
1 large egg
1 cup mashed potatoes

Canola oil, for deep-frying
½ pound lump crab meat
Panko bread crumbs, for breading
Kosher salt

In a small saucepan, combine the butter with ¼ cup water over high heat. When the water comes to a simmer and the butter is melted, add the flour. Reduce the heat to medium and stir until the resulting paste pulls away from the sides of the pan, 1 to 2 minutes. Remove from the heat. Allow to cool for 5 minutes. Add the egg to the pan and stir vigorously until the egg is incorporated into the flour mixture. Stir in the mashed potatoes and let cool.

Pour enough oil into a medium pot so that the oil comes 3 inches up the sides. Heat the oil to 350°F.

While the oil heats, gently fold the crab into the potato mixture; the lumpier the batter, the better. Using two soup spoons, shape the mixture into quenelles, or 2-inch footballs. (You should end up with about 35.) Roll in the panko. Deep-fry, working in batches and turning once, until crisp, brown, and heated through, 2 to 3 minutes. Drain on paper towels and season with salt.

LOLA FRIES WITH ROSEMARY

Rosemary on potatoes is so good, and hot crispy fries with rosemary and some sea salt are the best. I think of sea salt the way I do extra virgin-olive oil, as something to finish with. I use Maldon, which has a nice flaky texture.

There's no better way to ensure crispy fries than to fry them twice: first at 275°F and then later at 350°F. They crisp up even better on their final cook if they've been thoroughly chilled in the refrigerator. This means you can do the first fry well in advance of serving and pop them in the fridge. When you're ready, the fries take about two minutes to finish.

Serves 4

2 pounds russet potatoes
Canola oil, for deep-frying
1 teaspoon finely chopped fresh
   rosemary

1 teaspoon coarse sea salt

Peel the potatoes and cut them into long fries about ¼ inch thick. As you cut them, put them in a bowl of cold water to cover.

Pour enough oil into a medium pot so that the oil comes 3 inches up the sides. Heat the oil to 275°F.

Drain the fries and pat dry. Working in batches if necessary, cook them in the oil for about 5 minutes; they should be soft and pale. Remove them from the oil using a slotted spoon and rinse under cold water to remove excess oil and starch for a crisper fry later. Reserve the pot of oil.

Cover a rimmed baking sheet with paper towels and lay the fries on top. Chill completely in the refrigerator. The potatoes can be prepared this way up to a day in advance of cooking them.

Heat the oil to 350°F.

Add the fries, in batches, if necessary, to the oil and cook, stirring gently, until the fries are golden brown, about 5 minutes. Remove them from the oil to a large paper-towel-lined bowl and season them with the rosemary and salt, shaking the bowl to distribute the seasonings evenly.

Economy and Creativity

One of the great regrets of my early career was that I never traveled through Europe working in great kitchens in the countries my family comes from, where I might have learned even more deeply the food of my heritage. Of course, I love to travel in those countries and have eaten and explored well. But I didn't work there as a professional. And I've never worked for one of the big boys—one of those iconic chefs who have world-famous restaurants—in this country, either. You always wonder how life would be different.

For better or worse, everything I seem to have needed as a chef has been right here in Cleveland. Including my wife, Lizzie; she was the manager of Players when I got my first job out of culinary school in 1990. Following the Giovanni's debacle, and the horrible months "consulting," I landed an executive chef job at a tiny restaurant, the Caxton Café, owned by an architect and his wife who wanted to bring it beyond the small coffee-and-lunch, dinner-on-the-weekends type of spot it was. It had been open for about six months and they wanted to turn it into a bona fide restaurant. After about five months we began building up customers, so it was time to bring in my team. I called Liz Shanahan, who was still managing Players, and she agreed to be my GM, not realizing, of course, what she was getting into.

The dishwasher during my days at Players had been a teenager named Frank Rogers, who'd since then begun to cook. I called him, too, and he and I would cook together for the next seventeen years. The opening manager of Piccolo Mondo, where I'd had my first (and only) success, was a guy named Tim Bando. Tim came in as a server, and quickly realizing he loved restaurants but not people, began to join me in the kitchen; Tim is a chef at a restaurant in the Hamptons now but we still cook together when we can. Others would come aboard who are still with me today, are family, but that was the initial core Caxton team. Lizzie in front and me and two buddies in a kitchen so small there was no room to walk; we just stood in one place and cooked hard all night long. It was a tiny place, forty seats, and as it was in the center of the city and within walking distance of two stadiums and one indoor arena, we jammed all year.

Because the owners weren't restaurant people, I was free to cook whatever I wanted. This was my first experience creating an entire menu. Until then, it had been Mark's food at Player's or Italian food dictated by Carl at Piccolo Mondo. (And let's not forget about the Dover sole at Giovanni's!) Now I could do the food that I was passionate about. I loved big flavors, ginger and coriander, garlic and onions, chili peppers and sharp acidic ingredients like pickled ramps and turnips. But I also knew my audience. My city liked big chops and creamy pastas.

Because I did all the purchasing, I developed relationships with local farmers and began sourcing some of the great products being grown in and around Ohio. A guy named Patrick McCafferty showed up one day with some of the most beautiful watercress I'd ever seen. A young guy who'd farmed in California but who'd returned to his hometown to farm here, Patrick would soon be growing all kinds of lettuce and herbs and even raising lamb for me. Shortly after this, I met Doug Raubenolt, of Tea Hills Farm, in Loudonville, who to this day raises the tastiest chicken in Ohio, and Tom and Wendy Wiandt from Killbuck Valley Mushrooms.

As a small restaurant, we ran on a razor-thin margin so I really had to watch my costs. And because of the closet-size kitchen—one oven, four burners, and a small grill—I had to be efficient. My rule quickly became "If I can't finish a dish in two pans, preferably one, I won't do it."

I wanted to serve roasted duck breast, and my customers loved it, but it was so expensive that I'd have had to charge twenty-two dollars for an entrée, which in 1996 I knew was more than my customers would pay. So I came up with a second dish: I pulled the tenderloin off the duck breast, pounded it flat, and served it as a starter course of duck carpaccio for seven dollars. That way I could make money and still keep my prices low. Moreover, no one in Cleveland had heard of duck carpaccio, so the Caxton began to develop some cachet. When the local paper put me on the cover of its Sunday magazine, everyone in the city started paying attention to our little forty-seat restaurant.

So what I learned at the Caxton, above all, was the importance of economy, ingenuity, and creativity, never forgetting Mark Shary's soulful cooking and Carl's energy and drive and business smarts.

Looking back on it now, I realize just how lucky I was to have found these two mentors right out of school. School doesn't teach you passion; school teaches you technique. Once I had the technique, I could move on to the next step. Mark Shary taught me how to cook with passion, how to put your soul into food. Carl Quagliata taught me what it meant to be a restaurateur, how the front of the house and back of the house were connected and how the customer was always right, how to make the customer happy. I would leave the Caxton with the three pieces of the puzzle I needed in order to succeed: technique from the CIA, passion to cook from Mark, and know-how on running a restaurant from Carl.

Fish

Growing up in Cleveland, I rarely ate fish. We had fish fries on Lent, but that was about it, so fish is not a big part of my actual upbringing. That doesn't mean I haven't embraced it wholeheartedly, especially since it goes so well with my favorite seasonings.

The most common problem people have at home with fish is a tendency to overcook it. People think they don't want it to taste fishy, so they hammer it. But the more you cook fish, the fishier it tastes. You have to cook fish gently. Fish is really delicate and you've got to handle it with that in mind. A whole fish is great on the grill or roasted. Once it's filleted, you have to cook it in a pan. Sautéing or pan-roasting is perfect for fillets. I also like to poach fish, in a court bouillon, or in butter or olive oil. Poaching is a very delicate cooking method, and it keeps the fish moist. You need to treat fish like a woman—like a woman that you love, not a one-night stand.

Sautéing and Pan-Roasting

We use the sauté method for fish, tender cuts of meat, and vegetables—foods that don't need to be made tender from the cooking, foods that must be cooked relatively quickly, and foods that benefit from the additional flavor developed in the very high heat. It's a common method, but small variations in technique make a big difference.

The two most important factors in a good sauté are the heat of the pan and the movement, or lack thereof, of the food once it's in the pan.

Put your clean dry pan over medium to medium-high heat (a stainless-steel pan; I don't recommend nonstick pans for most preparations). Let it get hot. Smoke shouldn't be pouring off it, but it should be hot. Put your hand over it—don't touch it!—and you should be able to feel the heat. Add your oil or cooking fat, and give that time to heat up as well. When the oil is properly heated, you will see it rippling from the heat; for high-heat preparations—mushrooms, for example—you might want smoke just beginning to rise from the sides of the pan. Smoke indicates that the oil is as hot as it will get before beginning to break down (animal fats break down at lower temperatures than vegetable oils do).

Once the pan is hot and the oil is hot, add your seasoned fish or meat to the pan. Always pat it dry before you put it in the oil; it can sometimes be lightly dusted in flour to make it dry and to develop a better crust. If the fish or meat is wet, it will cool the oil and pan and you won't get a good sear, and your meat might stick to the pan.

As soon as you lay your food into the hot oil, don't do anything. Don't touch it, don't shake the pan. This is perhaps the biggest error people make when they sauté. As soon as it's in the fat, they want to start moving the food around. This commonly results in sticking and torn flesh. Allow the food to cook; it will develop a well-seared crust and pull naturally away from the pan if you don't touch it.

And that's all there is to sautéing: with a spatula flip the fish or meat and cook it until it's done.

I tend to cook fish at a lower temperature than meat (and granted, for low-temperature sautéing—delicate fish, say, or potato pancakes—a nonstick pan can be helpful). Fish cooked over very high heat seems to release oils that bring out an unpleasant fishy flavor. Most vegetables, too, benefit from a lower sauté temperature. Pork, lamb, beef, and veal benefit from very high heat.

A relative of the sauté is the pan-roast. This is one of the most common techniques used in restaurant cooking and is a great one to use at home. It's basically a combination of sauté and roast that's used for items that are tender but a little larger than those cuts of meat and fish for which sauté is best—thicker pieces of fish and meat, a fat fillet of grouper or a pork loin, for instance.

It starts out exactly like a sauté until it is flipped; once it's seared on one side, it's turned in the pan and then slid into a hot oven to finish cooking. Not only is the air surrounding the meat hot and helping the whole cut to cook evenly, but your stove, hands, and attention are freed up and can be turned to other work. At the restaurant, the ovens are turned to full blast to accommodate all the opening and closing throughout service. At home you can have a little more control over your oven temperature. Meats can go into an oven anywhere between 350° and 425°F. Fish, again, benefits from lower temperatures, 250°F or so. (If you can't put your pans in the oven because they have plastic handles, you need new pans with proper handles.)

When the food is cooked, either by the sauté or the pan-roast method, remove it from the heat. Fish is done at this point, but not meat. Cooked meat must rest so that the juices can redistribute themselves within the muscle and so that the temperature of the meat, which is concentrated on the surface, evens out throughout the meat. Resting is every bit as important to the cooking as the application of the heat. Make sure you allot time for it in your game plan. I recommend resting meat a few minutes per pound.

SLASH-AND-BURN GROUPER

This was another one of those cult-classic kind of dishes at Lola, so simple but so tasty: grouper seasoned inside with Jamaican jerk paste. It was just a theory for a long time, a dish that one of my good chef buddies, David Adjey, and I would talk about and wanted to try—slashing a piece of fish in the middle and putting something spicy inside. He does a similar dish with shrimp. At Lola we serve this fish with Crab Tater Tots (page 165), a crab guacamole, or a bell pepper salad.

Serves 6

6 6-ounce skin-on black grouper fillets
2 tablespoons Busha Browne's Jamaican Authentic Jerk Seasoning (see Symon Says)
1 teaspoon olive oil
Kosher salt
½ cup shrimp stock (see page 189) or Shellfish Stock (page 131)

Juice of 2 limes
4 tablespoons (½ stick) unsalted butter, cut into pieces
1 roasted red bell pepper, peeled, seeded, and finely diced
½ cup fresh cilantro leaves

Preheat the oven to 375°F.

Cut a pocket horizontally through the fish about 2 inches wide and 2 inches deep, and spread about a teaspoon of jerk seasoning in each fillet. Heat an ovenproof sauté pan over medium heat and when it is hot, add the olive oil. Pat the fillets dry with a paper towel (so that they won't stick to the pan), season lightly with salt, and lay them in the hot pan. Let the fish brown for 3 minutes and then gently turn them. Place the pan in the oven for 3 to 5 minutes, until the fish has reached an internal temperature of 140 °F.

Remove the pan from the oven and transfer the fillets to warm plates. Add the stock and lime juice to the pan, bring to a simmer, and reduce by half, 2 to 3 minutes. Remove from the heat and whisk in the butter and then the bell pepper. Pour over the fillets and garnish with cilantro leaves.

SYMON SAYS

I love jerk seasoning and used to make my own from a mixture of habaneros, cilantro, cumin, coriander, cinnamon, allspice, nutmeg, shallot, and garlic. But Busha Browne's Authentic Jerk Seasoning, available in grocery stores and specialty markets, is excellent for this dish.

BACON-WRAPPED PAN-ROASTED WALLEYE

In Cleveland we love our walleye, a rich white flavorful fish from the Great Lakes. When I was named one of the ten best new chefs in 1998 by *Food & Wine* magazine, they asked me for a recipe. I sent them one for walleye and it threw everyone off. New York fishmongers couldn't find it and they all wanted to call it walleyed pike. There is walleye and there is pike but it is not walleyed pike. Walleye is practically our native fish, and at Lola and Lolita restaurants it's always the biggest seller regardless of how it is prepared. Here I pair my favorite freshwater fish with my favorite meat.

Serves 4

8 3-ounce skinless walleye fillets
Kosher salt
1 teaspoon fresh thyme leaves

2 tablespoons unsalted butter, softened
16 strips bacon
1 tablespoon canola oil

Season the fillets with salt and sprinkle with the thyme. Rub one side of each of the fillets with the butter. Rest one fillet on another, buttered side to buttered side, to make four portions. Lay down 4 strips of bacon overlapping the strips. Arrange one portion of fish on top and wrap the bacon slices up and around the fish. Repeat with the remaining bacon and fish portions. Transfer to a large plate, cover with plastic wrap, and refrigerate for 1 hour.

Preheat the oven to 425°F.

Heat the oil in an ovenproof sauté pan over medium heat. Add the fish fillets to the pan seam side down and sauté the fillets to render the bacon, 3 to 4 minutes per side. Place the pan in the oven to crisp the bacon and finish cooking the fish, 2 to 4 minutes. Remove to a tray lined with paper towels to drain before serving.

SCALLOPS WITH LAMB SAUSAGE AND BEANS

I love the combination of lamb sausage with beans and some fresh mint. This dish can be made with shrimp instead of scallops and also can be the base for a roasted fish such as halibut or turbot. The fat of the sausage and acidity of the orange make a quick warm vinaigrette right in the pan. Scallops—like shrimp—are given size designations based on the number per pound. For this dish, I like scallops that are 1½ to 2 ounces a piece.

Serves 4 to 6

1 tablespoon olive oil
1 pound loose Lamb Sausage (page 105)
1 pound dry-packed scallops (preferably 12 U-10 scallops)
Kosher salt
1 fresno chile, seeded and diced

1 garlic clove, minced
1 shallot, minced
1 cup cooked cannellini beans
Grated zest and juice of 1 orange
1 cup Chicken Stock (page 131)
2 tablespoons torn fresh mint leaves

Heat the olive oil in a large skillet over medium heat. Add the crumbled lamb sausage and cook until slightly crispy, about 4 minutes. With a slotted spoon remove the sausage from the pan.

Increase the heat under the pan to medium-high. Season the scallops with salt and add them to the pan. Cook on the first side for 1 to 2 minutes or until golden brown. Flip the scallops, add the chili, garlic, and shallot, and continue to cook for 1 to 2 minutes.

Remove the scallops from the pan and return the sausage to the pan along with the beans, orange juice, and stock. Simmer for 3 minutes. Remove from the heat and divide the mixture among four to six bowls. Top with the scallops and then garnish with the orange zest and mint.

Poaching

Poaching is a gentle and controlled cooking method that is used often in restaurant kitchens and is easy to do at home. For a sauté, the pan is typically heated to 400°F or so. High temperatures are also used when roasting in the oven. And you need that high heat to create that delicious golden-brown crust on a roast chicken, that crisp sear on a cut of beef. But when you don't need that high-heat sear, poaching is by far the more effective cooking method. Water cannot rise above 212°F at its most vigorous boil. At just below a simmer, it's 180°F, a temperature that cooks food evenly and gently and keeps lean cuts of meat and fish very moist.

Additionally, poaching gives you a way to infuse flavor into what you are cooking by adding different seasonings to the liquid. I use two basic types of liquids for poaching. Most commonly, I opt for water to which I add aromatic vegetables, usually some kind of acid (vinegar or lemon juice), seasonings, and spice. In French, this is called a court bouillon, which translates roughly as "quick stock." I also occasionally poach in fat—butter or extra virgin olive oil—infused with bold aromatics.

OLIVE OIL–POACHED HALIBUT WITH FENNEL, ROSEMARY, AND GARLIC

This is a great poaching method for lean fish such as halibut, cod, or turbot, or for a lean meat like lamb or beef sirloin. It's easy to do well and is especially effective when flavoring with hard herbs such as rosemary (thyme and oregano are also excellent here).

This halibut would go well with many side dishes, such as Shaved Fennel Salad (see page 73), Grilled Radicchio (see page 157), Dad's Potato Pancakes (page 164), and Peas and Pancetta (page 147).

Serves 4

1 quart (4 cups) extra-virgin olive oil
2 garlic cloves, peeled
1 fennel bulb, quartered
3 sprigs of fresh rosemary

1 shallot, quartered
2 tablespoons kosher salt
1 tablespoon crushed red pepper flakes
4 6-ounce skinless halibut fillets

Combine the olive oil, garlic, fennel, rosemary, shallot, salt, and red pepper flakes in a 2-quart pan and bring the oil to a temperature of 140°F. Using a diffuser or by pulling the pan most of the way off the heat, maintain that temperature for about 20 minutes. You want to infuse the oil with the aromatics and red pepper flakes without really cooking them by letting the oil get too hot.

Submerge the halibut in the oil and poach until the fish reaches an internal temperature of 110°F, 15 to 20 minutes. Remove the fillets to paper towels to drain before serving.

SYMON SAYS

When poaching lamb and beef, remove the meat from the fat when it reaches between 120° and 130°F.

SALMON POACHED IN COURT BOUILLON

Court bouillon, a quick poaching liquid, is very easy to assemble and gives you a medium for spices and sweet aromatics. The method is simple: Bring all the ingredients to a simmer and then let them infuse. I strain the liquid before proceeding because it keeps the finished fish pristine.

This recipe uses a basic court bouillon, but if you want to take it in more complex directions, try one of these three flavor combinations:

- Cinnamon, cumin, coriander, and orange peel
- Rosemary, fennel, and crushed red pepper flakes
- Lemongrass, ginger, and coriander

The poached salmon goes with many side dishes. I love it with Braised Endive with Citrus (page 152) and Chickpeas and Skordalia (page 156). Chilled, it's great with Aioli (page 141).

Serves 4

1 carrot, coarsely chopped
1 onion, coarsely chopped
2 celery stalks, coarsely chopped
2 garlic cloves
1 bay leaf

2 tablespoons kosher salt
1 tablespoon black peppercorns
Juice of 3 lemons
4 6-ounce salmon fillets

Combine the carrot, onion, celery, garlic, bay leaf, salt, peppercorns, and lemon juice in a pot and add 1 quart (4 cups) water. Simmer for 30 minutes. Strain the liquid into a clean, wide, shallow pot.

Bring the court bouillon to 175°F over low heat. Submerge the salmon fillets in it. Using an instant-read thermometer, keep an eye on the temperature of the liquid to make sure you don't let the temperature drop too low. On the other hand, if it begins to simmer, it's too high. Remove the salmon when it feels medium-firm when poked, 7 to 10 minutes. It should be rare to medium-rare in the center, 110°F. Remove the fillets to paper towels to drain before serving.

BUTTER-POACHED WILD SALMON WITH SHALLOTS AND THYME

This is the poaching method that yields the most delicious results, but it is also the most difficult because you must keep the butter emulsified—that is, you must keep it from breaking (when the fat separates from the water and whey and solids). But once you master this, your possibilities are endless. It's a great method for lean fish, but also for lean meats and even rich meats, as well as for vegetables such as asparagus and peas.

This preparation calls for two pounds of butter, most of which will be left over after your fish is done. It can be strained, refrigerated, and reused two more times for poaching fish, or you can use it to whisk into sauces for other fish dishes, such as the Slash-and-Burn Grouper (page 175), or to toss with blanched vegetables.

Side dishes to serve with butter-poached salmon include Fried Brussels Sprouts with Walnuts and Capers (page 155) and Seared Wild Mushrooms (page 158).

Serves 4

Juice of 4 oranges
Juice of 1 lemon
2 sliced shallots
2 garlic cloves
4 sprigs of fresh thyme

2 bay leaves
2 tablespoons kosher salt
2 pounds unsalted butter, cubed and chilled
4 6-ounce skinless salmon fillets

Pour the orange and lemon juices into a nonreactive saucepan and simmer over medium heat to reduce by a third, 5 to 10 minutes. Add the shallots, garlic, thyme, bay leaves, and salt. Return the liquid to a gentle simmer and whisk in the butter a few cubes at a time until they're all incorporated, whisking continuously.

Bring the butter to 130°F—using an instant read thermometer to gauge the temperature—and adjust the heat to maintain this temperature. Submerge the salmon and poach it until it reaches an internal temperature of 110°F, 15 to 25 minutes. Remove the fillets to paper towels to drain before serving.

GRILLED RED SNAPPER
WITH GRAPE LEAVES AND AVGOLEMONO

This snapper gets briefly marinated in lemon and olive oil, wrapped in brined grape leaves, then grilled, and it's served with a traditional Greek sauce of egg and lemon. Simple preparation, bold straightforward flavors—a simple, fantastic dish.

I love grape leaves, and my favorite way to use them is with fish on the grill. Any fish can be wrapped in grape leaves; they give the fish a briny flavor that reinforces its oceany background. They also help to keep the fish moist and protect it from charring. The grape leaves pick up some char, however, and this really enhances their flavor. Any lean meat would benefit from this treatment. I've sometimes wrapped lamb loin in grape leaves.

I prefer buying jarred brined grape leaves imported from Greece rather than brining my own; it's hard to find leaves that are tender enough. You can purchase jarred grape leaves in supermarkets and specialty grocery stores, or they can be ordered online (see Sources, page 250).

Serves 4

2 2-pound red snappers, scaled and
    gutted
2 lemons, halved
2 tablespoons chopped fresh oregano
    leaves
¾ cup olive oil
Kosher salt

20 grape leaves (from 1 16-ounce jar)
1 cup shrimp stock (see page 189) or
    Shellfish Stock (page 131)
1 garlic clove, minced
1 large egg
2 large egg yolks

Cut four horizontal slits down each side, through the skin and into the flesh, of each snapper.

Juice 1 lemon and whisk the juice together with the oregano and half of the olive oil.

Salt each fish liberally and place in a nonreactive container. Pour the lemon-oregano marinade over the fish and let it sit at room temperature for 30 minutes, turning once during that time.

On a work surface, lay out 10 grape leaves, making sure to overlap them to make a "sheet" that is as wide as the fish and long enough to wrap around it one and a half times. Roll one fish in the grape leaves. Repeat to wrap the other fish.

Light a medium-hot fire in your grill.

In a 2-quart saucepan, combine the remaining lemon halves, the stock, and the

recipe continued on next page

garlic and bring to a simmer. Remove from the heat. Whisk together the egg and yolks and then whisk into the stock mixture.

Return the pan to the stovetop over low heat and stir the sauce until it thickens, 2 to 3 minutes. Make sure you stir constantly and that the sauce doesn't get too hot; if it simmers, the eggs will scramble. When the sauce is thickened, take it off the heat and set it in a warm spot on the stove.

Brush the fish with the remaining olive oil. Place the fish on the grill and cook for 4 minutes per side, making sure not to burn the grape leaves, until the fish is cooked through. Remove the fish from the grill, place on a serving plate, and top with the sauce.

SYMON SAYS

Cooking whole fish on the bone is the easiest way to cook fish at home! The fish stays moist so there's less danger of overcooking it, and cooking it on the bone enhances the fish's natural sweetness. Look for 1- to 2-pound varieties of walleye, whitefish, trout, striped bass, or snapper.

The Power of the Hot Vinaigrette

When we think of vinaigrette we almost always think of an oil-and-vinegar-based dressing for cold preparations—salads, greens, or cold vegetables. And of course a vinaigrette is great in such cases. But what I love most is to finish a hot dish, a fish or a meat, with a vinaigrette I've made right there in the pan.

You'll see this simple technique used throughout this book: vinaigrettes on pork chops and lamb chops, on scallops with sausage, on pork belly with watermelon, on fried Brussels sprouts. And even when I don't call something a vinaigrette, there's invariably some acidic ingredient that serves the same purpose. In this chapter, you'll find a straightforward vinaigrette on a simple preparation of sautéed shrimp (page 189).

I've never relied too much on stocks and stock-based sauces. They too easily become over-reduced and sticky on the tongue. Stocks are also time-consuming. We're always making stock at the restaurant—and when I do use them, it's because they're vital. And I don't tend to make a lot of stock at home. When saucing food, I almost always turn to a vinaigrette.

Cold vinaigrettes are excellent, but add one to the hot pan you've sautéed some shrimp in, and the blended acid and oil will pick up all the flavor of the bits of protein and sugars that have stuck to the pan. Toss in some herbs, adjust the seasoning, and you're done. You're combining all the elements of a classic sauce, but instead of taking a long time, it all comes together *à la minute*.

A word about vinaigrettes generally: The classic vinaigrette ratio is 3 to 1, three parts oil to one part vinegar. But I've always found that to be a little flat. You don't really need all that oil; to me it makes a dish unnecessarily heavy. Instead, I start a vinaigrette with a 1 to 1 ratio, equal parts acid and fat, and then gradually increase the fat until it tastes right. The strength is dependent on two things: what I'm putting it on and the type of acid being used. Is it a sharp red wine vinegar, a milder sherry vinegar, or a sweet balsamic? If I'm using citrus, is it orange juice, which is relatively low in acid and very sweet, or is it lime juice, which is sharper even than lemon juice? Taste, taste, taste. You've always got to be tasting.

I use the hot vinaigrette technique all the time at the restaurants, and it's a perfect strategy for the home cook. Learn the technique with one dish, and then apply it to virtually any sauté you wish, fish or meat or vegetable. Alter your acid, and vary your herb—mint, basil, parsley, whatever you wish. The technique is quick, it uses ingredients that are at hand, and, most important, its results are really delicious.

SHRIMP WITH DILL VINAIGRETTE

This is a simple shrimp and garlic sauté: The shrimp are quickly seared and garlic is added, followed by a little bit of wine to finish cooking them and to begin the sauce. A quick stock made from the shells of the shrimp and a warm vinaigrette ties everything together. Make the vinaigrette just before sautéing the shrimp so that the dill doesn't discolor.

Serves 4 as a starter or 2 as a main course

Shrimp

½ onion, thinly sliced
½ carrot, thinly sliced
1 teaspoon canola oil
2 slices peeled fresh ginger, each the size of a quarter
1 teaspoon coriander seeds, toasted (see Symon Says, page 69)
½ bay leaf, crumbled

1 pound large (12- to 16-count) shrimp, peeled and deveined, shells reserved
2 tablespoons olive oil
Kosher salt
2 garlic cloves, sliced
¼ cup dry white wine
1 tablespoon salt-packed capers, rinsed and drained

Dill vinaigrette

1 shallot, minced
Kosher salt
Grated zest and juice of 2 lemons

2 tablespoons chopped fresh dill
½ cup extra-virgin olive oil

In a small saucepan over medium heat, sweat the onion and carrot in the canola oil until softened, 2 minutes. Add the ginger, coriander, bay leaf, and shrimp shells and cook until the shrimp shells are pink. Add 2 cups water and bring to a simmer. Simmer on low for 15 to 20 minutes while you prepare the dill vinaigrette. When you're ready to cook the shrimp, strain the stock through a fine-mesh strainer into a measuring cup. You'll need ½ cup.

To make the vinaigrette, combine the shallot in a bowl with a pinch of salt. Add the lemon zest and juice and the dill. Whisk in the extra-virgin olive oil and add more salt if needed.

To cook the shrimp, heat the 2 tablespoons of olive oil in a large sauté pan over medium heat. Season the shrimp with salt, add them to the pan, and cook for about 2 minutes per side. Add the garlic and cook for 1 minute. Deglaze the pan with the white wine. Add the ½ cup stock, bring it to a simmer—making sure to scrape any particles off the bottom of the pan with a wooden spoon—and let it reduce for 1 minute.

Divide the shrimp among plates. Add the capers to the pan, whisk in the vinaigrette just to heat through, and pour the pan sauce over the shrimp.

"Dad, I Need to Borrow Three Hundred Bucks"

The Caxton Café was the hardest reservation in the city as we entered the new year, 1997; we were jamming, and I was doing great food the way I wanted while running the financials efficiently. I'd fallen in love with Liz and her seven-year-old son, Kyle. Frank and Tim were solid in the kitchen and the front of the house staff had coalesced into the wonderful dysfunctional family that restaurants can become. I was in a kind of culinary nirvana, completely at peace, everything was perfect.

Except for that nagging little piece of the puzzle that wasn't there yet. We were making a lot of money for the owners of the restaurant; we'd quadrupled sales. My goal, and now with Liz, our goal, was to own our own restaurant. When it was clear that the owners wouldn't let us buy the Caxton or even give us equity—why would the owners sell or give a piece of this suddenly successful business if they didn't have to?—I talked to some restaurateurs who were looking to open a new restaurant and needed a chef partner. I gave the Caxton my six-weeks notice—and they let me go four days later. Which would have been fine except for a little glitch: The new restaurant deal fell through.

So it was back to consulting, being miserable, and having no idea what was in store for us. Within weeks, though, Liz's sister heard word on the street that Bohemia, a funky little restaurant in the neighborhood I'd been living in for five years, a semiurban enclave called Tremont, on the edge of Cleveland's industrial Flats, was for sale. I found the owner immediately; it was true, the place, the appliances, the liquor license, it was all for sale. Lizzie and I talked it over. We talked with family, we spoke with a regular customer at Caxton who'd long said to contact him if we wanted to do something on our own, and we decided to go for it. Her name would be Lola, the name of a close and ebullient family friend and a name we just loved.

We didn't want to be beholden to investors, so we determined we'd open the restaurant ourselves. In the end, we came up with $170,000 dollars from family and a friend. That was what we had and that was what we used. We did just about everything ourselves, and we created a new restaurant. One hundred seventy grand: hard to believe today that you could open a restaurant for that little money. Small as it seems now, it was nevertheless a lot to us; it was all we had. As soon as every penny was gone, we had no choice but to open for business. We had nothing in the bank—nothing; we were flat broke by March 1997. Liz, my buddy Chris, and I were still hanging lights when the first customers walked in. When my mom arrived, she started to cry because we were so behind.

We'd just open soft, on Wednesday, real soft and quiet to see how things would go. Just tell a few friends. We didn't know if everything would work. About midday, Liz and I realized we had no cash, not a dollar bill to put in the till. We needed cash to accept cash, make change. The conversation went something like this.

"Dad, I need to borrow three hundred bucks." He'd already lent us a serious amount.

"What for?"

"We need some money in the cash register to make change."

"So go to the bank."

"Dad, please, I don't have time to go to the bank!"

"There's an ATM down the street."

"Dad, please!"

I couldn't bear to tell him that we'd drained the accounts to nothing. Couldn't do it. He gave me the cash, and we opened for business.

I don't know how the word spread, but Lola filled up that night. I don't really remember how the night ended, or what happened during that first week. I only remember Lizzie coming around into the open kitchen that first night, while I was cooking, and whispering to me, incredulous, "Michael, we just did a thousand dollars in the first hour!"

Lola was jammed the next night and the night after that. The people and the cash began to flow. We were still poor, and Lizzie was purchasing wine by the bottle and not the case— two bottles at a time, one if they were expensive—but we were lucky and I kept cooking and the people kept coming. And in a little more than four years, we'd paid everyone back. Even my dad.

BRAISED SWORDFISH COLLAR
WITH CHORIZO AND CLAMS

The "collar" is a section of the fish, between the head and the body, close to the spine, that's very rich and fatty, so you can thoroughly cook this cut and it remains very flavorful and juicy. The collar is the best part of this big fish and it's hard to find, so you'll have to make nice with your fishmonger to get it. You can substitute swordfish loin.

David Burke, probably the most imitated chef in America in the 1980s and '90s, popularized this cut. He used to grill it. I like to braise it, cook it all the way through. Once you have the collar it's hard to go wrong. It's served here with clams and chorizo and a little tomato broth.

Serves 6

2 tablespoons olive oil
6 6-ounce pieces swordfish from the
    collar or loin
Kosher salt
1 yellow onion, minced
2 garlic cloves, minced
1 fennel bulb, cut into medium dice
1 serrano chile, minced
1 carrot, cut into medium dice
½ pound smoked chorizo, cut into ¼-inch
    pieces

½ cup sherry
1 small pinch of saffron
1 cup Chicken Stock (page 131)
1 12-ounce can crushed whole peeled
    tomatoes, with their juice
1½ pounds middleneck clams (about 24),
    well washed
2 tablespoons chopped kalamata olives
3 tablespoons chopped fresh flat-leaf
    parsley leaves
3 tablespoons sliced fresh basil leaves

Preheat the oven to 375°F.

In a 7- or 8-quart enameled cast-iron Dutch oven, heat the oil over medium-high heat. Season the swordfish with salt, add it to the pan, and brown it, about 2 minutes per side. Add the onion, garlic, fennel, chili, and carrot; lower the heat to medium; and cook to sweat the vegetables, about 2 minutes. Add the chorizo and continue to sweat. Pour in the sherry and bring to a simmer, scraping the bottom of the pot. Add the saffron, stock, tomatoes, and clams and bring to a simmer.

Cover the pot and place it in the oven for 15 minutes, or until the clams open. (Discard any clams that do not open.) Remove from the oven, add the olives, parsley, and basil, and serve.

Meat

I am a carnivore for so many reasons. I love meat for its texture. I love . . . eating flesh. Fish and vegetables, they don't have that chew. I love cutting into a big rib-eye steak or a grilled pork chop. I love a charred outside combined with a beautiful fleshy center. I love the fat. With so many other foods, all other foods, fish and vegetables, you have to add fat. Not meat; it's got the fat built into it, it's got that flavor and richness built into it.

Meat is very easy to cook well, if you remember a few points. Most cooks, most home cooks especially, start cooking it when it's too cold. Meat is very dense and you should let it come to room temperature before cooking it. (Is that important to do with fish? Yes, to an extent. It should temper a little. But it's twice as important to do with meat.) The bigger a cut is, the more important tempering it is. If you don't let the meat come to room temperature, it's never going to cook correctly.

The next thing to acknowledge is how important it is to season it well in advance, so that the seasoning penetrates it, which takes time, and to allow the salt to begin to change the cell structure a little to ensure that you have a very juicy cooked piece of meat with great depth of flavor. You almost can't salt meat too early. I like to salt it eight to twenty-four hours before cooking it, storing it covered in the refrigerator.

And then, cooking it; there are so many ways to cook it. The main question here is simple: Is it a tender piece of meat that doesn't need some form of tenderizing? If so, it can be cooked quickly over high heat. Or is it a heavily worked muscle and therefore tough? In this case, it requires some form of tenderization, usually by long cooking at a low temperature.

And finally, resting, which is every bit as important as proper cooking. Meat needs to rest, to allow the very hot exterior temperature to equalize with the internal temperature and to let the juices spread out within the meat. Don't cover it.

Because meat is so rich, because it has this built-in fat and flavor, I spend most of my energy adding enough acidity to the dish to balance that richness, whether with a vinaigrette or with a pickled vegetable or a salad. The greatest example is the salsa verde (see page 239), which goes very well with pretty much any meat. And that's all there is to it. Season it in advance, let it come to room temperature, cook it properly, let it rest, and balance its richness with acidity . . . as all of the following recipes demonstrate.

Roasting and Grilling

Roasting is what we do to larger cuts of meat. It would be difficult to sauté a leg of lamb or a whole chicken. You've got to roast the big cuts so that they're evenly cooked, and, in most cases, this requires using heat high enough for the meat to develop a tasty exterior. But the time and temperature varies from one cut to the next. For some items, you want a very hot oven—400°F and higher for roast chicken, for instance. For a large dense muscle, such as a rib roast, you might want a low temperature to ensure that the interior is cooked before the exterior is overcooked.

You'd never roast fish fillets (these must be sautéed or grilled), but whole fish, on the bone, is excellent roasted at a medium temperature. In some instances you want varying temperatures: with the rib roast or a leg of lamb, you might want to start it in a very hot oven or on a hot grill to develop a delicious exterior, then cook it through slowly with more moderate heat.

Last but not least, vegetables can be delicious roasted. Roasting vegetables at very high temperatures allows them to caramelize (to release some of their sugars and brown) and to develop more complex flavors. Any sturdy vegetable—broccoli, cauliflower, asparagus, green beans, Brussels sprouts—can be roasted with excellent results.

Grilling is a great technique that can mirror sautéing, pan-roasting, or roasting. Like those stove preparations, grilling is a "dry-heat" technique, meaning water is not part of the cooking medium, and the same rules apply. For tender cuts—a lamb chop, for instance—high-heat grilling gives a good sear, resulting in a flavorful exterior. Build a hot fire and cook the item directly over the coals—that is, over direct heat. For larger items that you might otherwise roast, grill over indirect heat. Do this by building a fire on one side of your grill; sear a spatchcocked chicken or a roast over direct heat, then move it to the other side of the grill and cover it to finish the cooking.

Let your coals get hot before you start cooking (and yes, cook over wood coals or charcoal; as far as I'm concerned, grilling over gas is like kissing your sister). After spreading the coals out and putting your grill grate on, give the grate time to heat up as well. I often rub the grate with a towel soaked with oil and give the meat I'm cooking a coating of oil as well, which promotes even cooking and prevents sticking. But again, the key is to let your grate get very hot for anything you intend to sear.

I love grilling not only for the big flavors it brings to food, but also because it's an active form of cooking. You've got to pay attention and respond throughout the process.

MUSHROOM-STUFFED BRICK-ROASTED CHICKEN

This recipe uses boned half chickens. It's easiest to order these from your butcher: Request two small birds, under three pounds each if possible, and ask for the breast and leg meat to be kept together—attached to a single piece of skin, that is—for the end two joints of the wing to be removed, and for the drumstick meat to be kept intact for each half. (I include instructions for doing this yourself in the Symon Says note. If you like to butcher, this is fun; if you don't, you may find this a bit difficult.) Alternatively, you can substitute skin-on boneless chicken breast halves.

The mushrooms do many things in this preparation. They form an interior garnish for the meat; they perfume the meat; they prevent the breast meat from drying out as the leg meat requires longer cooking; and they release their own juices as the chicken rests. Placing hot bricks on the chicken contributes to the short cooking time.

I recommend serving this on a bed of Red Potatoes with Arugula (page 163), removing the chicken directly from the oven onto the potatoes so that you retain all the juices the mushrooms and chicken release during the five-minute rest.

Serves 4

4 2½-pound chickens, halved and boned, or 4 8-ounce skin-on, boneless breast halves
½ recipe Seared Wild Mushrooms (page 158)

Kosher salt and freshly ground black pepper
2 tablespoons olive oil

Preheat the oven to 425°F. Wrap 4 bricks in aluminum foil and place them in the oven.

Arrange a boned chicken half flesh side up on your cutting board. Lift the tenderloin from the breast and deepen the crease where it rests by pushing on it with your index finger. Stuff this area with some mushrooms, then fold the tenderloin back over the stuffing. (If using chicken breast halves instead, the process is the same.) Stuff the thigh and leg meat with mushrooms. Repeat with the other three chicken halves. Season them all liberally with salt and pepper.

Heat 2 large ovenproof skillets over medium-high heat and add a tablespoon of oil to each. Put the chickens into the hot pans skin side down, top each with a brick, and cook for 7 to 10 minutes. Remove the bricks, flip the chickens, and roast in the oven until the temperature in the thickest part of the thigh reaches 160°F, 7 to 10 minutes. Remove the birds from the oven and let the chickens rest for 5 minutes before serving.

SYMON SAYS

To bone the chickens yourself: Start by slicing along one side of the keel bone, the central bone that divides the breast halves. Continue to cut following the rib cage and capturing as much meat as possible. Slice your knife down along the wishbone and through the wing joint, which will separate the breast meat and the wing from the carcass. Next, find the joint where the thigh attaches to the carcass and cut through that, being careful to keep the leg and breast together (they're attached only by the skin at this point). Bring your knife blade down the length of thigh bone on the flesh side of the thigh, cutting the bone away from the flesh, and cut through the joint attaching it to the drumstick. Remove the thigh bone. Next, cut right around the leg bone (drumstick), starting at the thigh end, with the goal of freeing the bone from the meat and skin of the drumstick; using a paper towel to get a good grip, pull the bone out through the drumstick meat (you may want to chop off the joint at the fleshy end of the drumstick to facilitate its popping through). Remember, you want to keep the drumstick meat whole so that you can easily stuff mushrooms inside. Now you're all set.

VEAL CHOP MILANESE WITH ARUGULA SALAD

This is a very simple dish to make and is also one that works with all sorts of different meats, such as chicken, pork, beef, and most game. It makes a great late lunch or early dinner in the summertime when tomatoes and arugula are bountiful. The thing I love about it is you get some great texture from the standard breading, and the arugula salad keeps things light and flavorful.

Serves 4

4 bone-in veal chops, each 12 ounces
2 cups all-purpose flour
4 large eggs
2 cups panko bread crumbs
½ cup grated Parmesan cheese
Kosher salt and freshly ground black
   pepper
¼ cup olive oil

2 tablespoons unsalted butter
1 garlic clove, minced
Juice of 1 lemon
¼ cup extra-virgin olive oil
1 red onion, thinly sliced
3 cups arugula
1 cup grape tomatoes, halved
12 fresh basil leaves

Put the veal chops on a cutting board and cover them with a large piece of plastic wrap. With a meat mallet, pound the meat to ¼ inch thick.

Set up a breading station: In three separate bowls put the flour, eggs, and bread crumbs. Lightly whisk the eggs. Stir the Parmesan into the bread crumbs.

Season the veal chops liberally with salt and pepper. Dredge them in flour and shake off the excess, then dip them in egg, and then in bread crumbs to coat.

Heat a large sauté pan over medium heat and add the olive oil and butter. When the fat is hot add the veal chops and cook until golden brown, 4 to 6 minutes per side. Remove to paper towels to drain until ready to serve.

In a large mixing bowl combine the garlic, lemon juice, and 1 teaspoon salt. Whisk in the extra-virgin olive oil. Add the onion, toss to coat evenly, and let marinate for 10 minutes.

Add the arugula, tomatoes, and basil to the dressing and gently toss together.

To serve, place a veal chop in the center of each plate and top with salad.

GRILLED LAMB T-BONES WITH FAVA BEAN SALAD

I fire up the grill for this recipe on the first week the weather breaks; this dish screams spring. I often serve grilled dishes with chilled or room-temperature salads, and this is a great example. I especially love this one, which is loaded with favas, feta, and olives. Don't be shy with the vinegar and extra-virgin olive oil, either. It's not only the dressing for the salad but also the sauce for the lamb; using a vinaigrette to sauce the salad and the meat is a frequent feature of Greek cuisine, and I find the pairing of grilled meat, vegetables, and vinaigrette unbeatable. For the biggest flavor, I recommend seasoning the lamb a day before cooking.

Serves 4 to 8

Lamb
8 lamb T-bones, each 1 inch thick
1 teaspoon kosher salt
Freshly ground black pepper
1 tablespoon coriander seeds, toasted and
    crushed (see Symon Says, page 69)
½ teaspoon crushed red pepper flakes
¼ teaspoon sugar

Fava Bean Salad
2 pounds fresh fava beans in the pods
3 pickled fresno chilies (see page 120),
    sliced in ¼-inch rings
2 garlic cloves, minced
⅓ cup fresh mint leaves
⅓ cup sliced kalamata olives
⅓ cup crumbled feta cheese
6 tablespoons red wine vinegar
¾ cup extra-virgin olive oil
½ teaspoon kosher salt
½ teaspoon cracked black pepper

Sprinkle both sides of each lamb chop with the salt, pepper, coriander, red pepper flakes, and sugar. Cover and refrigerate for 24 hours.

Remove the lamb from the refrigerator 30 minutes before cooking. Build a hot fire in your grill. Bring a medium pot of water to a boil. While the water is heating, shell the fava beans. Add enough salt to the water that it tastes like the ocean (about a cup per gallon). When the water returns to a boil, add the favas and cook until tender, about 2 minutes. Drain and run under cold water to cool. Drain well and then pinch the favas out of their skins. In a large bowl, combine the favas with the chilies, garlic, mint, olives, feta, vinegar, olive oil, salt, and pepper and toss to combine.

Grill the lamb chops until they're just past medium rare, 2 to 4 minutes per side.

Remove the chops to a platter and top with the fava bean salad.

GRILLED HANGER STEAK
WITH STEAK SAUCE AND PICKLED CHILIES

This classic French bistro cut, the hanger, is also referred to as onglet or butcher's steak. It hangs right below the diaphragm of the steer, and there is only one per animal. The reason it is called the butcher's steak is because while everyone else is eating the flavorless tenderloin, the butcher is chowing down on this super-flavorful cut. Yes, you have to cut it against the grain and yes, you will have to chew, but trust me—it is all worth it when you bite into this delicious muscle. Leave the pricey tenderloins for the suckers and buy some hangers. You'll quickly realize what the butchers have known all along: This steak rocks.

Lola Steak Sauce, a reduction of balsamic, red wine vinegar, anchovies, garlic, and spices, has good acidity and sweetness to help balance the deep rich flavors of the meat. Pickled chilies contribute acidity too, as well as some heat. Because the hanger has such strong flavor, with notes of iron and liver, it needs these intense contrasting notes.

Serves 6

1 tablespoon kosher salt
1 teaspoon sugar
1 teaspoon coriander seeds, crushed
1 teaspoon ancho chile powder
4 pounds hanger steak, trimmed of fat
  and connective tissue

½ cup extra-virgin olive oil
1 cup pickled chilies (page 120), sliced
½ cup pickled onions (see page 117)
1 cup fresh flat-leaf parsley leaves
Lola Steak Sauce (page 134)

Combine the salt, sugar, coriander, and chile powder in a small bowl and coat the steaks with the mixture. Refrigerate overnight or for up to 2 days.

Remove the steaks from the refrigerator 30 minutes before you want to cook them.

Build a hot fire in your grill. Brush the steaks with half the olive oil and grill them for 3 minutes per side for medium rare. Remove from the grill and let rest, uncovered, for 10 minutes.

While the steaks are resting, in a medium bowl toss the pickled chilies, onions, parsley, and remaining olive oil together.

Slice the steaks against the grain, divide among six plates, and top with the salad and a drizzle of steak sauce.

Braising

Braising is a two-part process used for tougher cuts of meat, muscles that are heavily worked—from the belly, shoulder, shanks, cheeks—and therefore develop a lot of connective tissue that must be broken down before the meat gets tender. The first part of the process is to sear the meat, which creates flavor and texture and begins to set the protein, so that blood and other proteins aren't released to coagulate and compromise your cooking liquid. The second part is a long, low cook in liquid. As with all fundamental cooking methods, there are many finer points that distinguish an excellent braise from an average braise.

Seasoning—always be thinking about seasoning. It's important, both for flavor and texture, to season your meat with salt and any other spices in advance.

Searing—flouring meat is important for the best possible sear. It ensures the outside of the meat is dry when it is put into the hot fat (moisture cools the fat down, slowing or even preventing browning) and helps to create a good surface. Be sure to shake all the excess flour off the meat before putting it into the hot oil; any that falls off the meat will remain in the oil and burn. And don't crowd the pan with meat—if it's crowded the meat will only steam and therefore won't be able to brown.

For the second part of the process, I think first about my cooking liquid. Never miss an opportunity to build flavors: Begin the second phase by sweating or caramelizing vegetables that will fortify the cooking liquid, seasoning them as you go. When the aromatics and any other ingredients, say tomato paste for color and flavor, are cooked, then, if I'm using wine, I add it here to deglaze the pan, scraping up the flavorful browned bits from the bottom. I then add the stock and often some acid such as red wine vinegar, followed by the meat. I bring this to a simmer, then cover the pan and put it in a low oven, ideally about 225°F. (You can go as high as 325°F; this will speed the cooking somewhat.)

Part of what defines a braise is that the meat isn't entirely submerged in the liquid, that the third of it that's above the surface is allowed to brown a little deeper than what's below the surface, adding another layer of flavor.

I like to remove the cover during the last half hour or so of cooking, to further brown the exposed surface of the meat and to reduce the cooking liquid to a flavorful sauce.

The meat is done when it's tender—often referred to as fork tender, meaning it gives no resistance when you stick a fork or knife into it. The pot is then removed from the heat and the meat is left to cool in its own braising liquid. You could eat it immediately, but, for a number of reasons, braised dishes are best a day or so after they've cooked. Cooling the liquid allows the fat to rise and congeal on the surface, where it can easily be removed; the meat reabsorbs some of the cooking liquid as it cools; and flavors continue to develop during the cooling phase.

Once the braise is thoroughly chilled, the meat can be removed from the cooking liquid and that liquid can be adjusted for its final use as the sauce for the braise. You have the opportunity here to reduce it a little more, adjust its seasoning, and adjust its texture, whether by straining out the solids for a very refined sauce or by puréeing it for a thicker sauce or leaving the aromatic vegetables whole for a more rustic finished dish.

BRAISED VEAL SHANK WITH GREMOLATA

Like the pot roast, this is another of those fundamental braised dishes, but I like to jazz it up it with some gremolata. Many people serve this kind of dish with something rich, such as mashed potatoes; traditionally in Italy this would be served with a saffron risotto. But I think it's a mistake to pair rich with rich in most cases.

Endive is a perfect side for this winter dish: It's available in cold months and adds a bitter edge to the rich veal and sauce as well as some sweetness developed in the braising process. Gremolata—lemon zest, garlic, and parsley, all of it minced—is a classic garnish for this and many other braises.

Serves 6

Veal Shanks

¾ cup brine-cured green olives

6 2-inch-thick veal shank pieces

Kosher salt and freshly ground black pepper

All-purpose flour, for dredging

2 tablespoons olive oil

1 tablespoon unsalted butter

1 medium-large onion, halved lengthwise and thinly sliced

3 garlic cloves, minced

1 salt-packed anchovy fillet, rinsed and chopped

Grated zest of 2 lemons

1½ tablespoons salt-packed capers, rinsed and drained

3 sprigs of fresh rosemary

1½ cups dry white wine

1½ cups Chicken Stock (page 131)

Braised Endive with Citrus (page 152)

Gremolata

¼ cup finely chopped fresh flat-leaf parsley leaves

1 tablespoon freshly grated lemon zest

1½ teaspoons minced garlic, or to taste

Preheat the oven to 275°F.

To make the veal, lightly crush the olives with the side of a large knife and discard the pits. Finely chop a third of them and set aside.

Pat the veal shanks dry with paper towels and season with salt and pepper. Dredge each shank in flour and shake off the excess. In a 12-inch heavy sauté pan, heat 1 tablespoon of the oil and the butter over medium-high heat until the foam subsides. Brown both sides of the shanks in batches, about 2 minutes on each side. Transfer the shanks to a roasting pan.

Wipe out the sauté pan and add the remaining tablespoon of oil. Add the onion and cook over medium heat, stirring, until golden, 5 to 10 minutes. Add the garlic and anchovy and cook, stirring, for 1 minute. Add the olives, lemon zest, capers, rosemary, and wine and simmer for 5 minutes. Add the stock and return the liquid to a simmer. Pour over the shanks and cover the roasting pan tightly with foil. Reduce the oven temperature to 225°F and braise the shanks in the oven for 4 to 6 hours, or until the meat is very tender. If desired, let the shanks cool before covering and refrigerating for up to 2 days. Discard the fat from the top before reheating.

To make the gremolata, combine the parsley, zest, and garlic in a small bowl.

Transfer the shanks with a slotted spoon to another roasting pan or deep oven-proof platter and keep warm, covered, in the oven. Strain the cooking liquid through a sieve into a 1-quart (4-cup) glass measuring cup and reserve the solids, discarding the rosemary. Let the liquid stand until the fat rises to the top; skim and discard the fat. (There should be about 1½ cups liquid. If necessary, in a saucepan simmer the liquid until it is reduced to 1½ cups.) Add the reserved solids to the liquid, heat through, stir in the reserved olives, and pour over the shanks.

Serve the shanks on top of the braised endive, sprinkled with the gremolata.

BRAISED RABBIT THIGHS WITH OLIVES AND ORANGE

In culinary school, I discovered I was allergic to rabbit, but I loved it so much that I kept eating little bits until my head stopped swelling up. (This is probably not the medically recommended way to handle a food allergy, so either consult your doc first or don't hold me responsible if things don't work out so well! Or, make this with chicken thighs.) In any case, I was primed when the Chairman revealed "Battle Rabbit" during my first season on *Iron Chef.* We used a pressure cooker to make the tough thighs tender in under an hour, but at home or at the restaurant I would simply braise them. The pressure cooker really cuts cooking time, but it has drawbacks: You can't use your senses of sight and touch and you can't test for doneness. I'm a fan of low and slow because it's gentle on the meat.

Orange and olives always play well together and are a combination I love. Add a little shaved fennel and mint and you've got yourself a salad. I love a rich piece of protein with a salad—grilled lamb on favas and mint, spicy greens on a steak—and this is another example.

Serves 6

12 bone-in rabbit thighs or chicken thighs (about 3 pounds)
Kosher salt and freshly ground black pepper
3 tablespoons coriander seeds, toasted and ground (see Symon Says, page 69; 2 tablespoons)
½ cup all-purpose flour
¼ cup olive oil, or more as needed
1 medium red onion, halved and sliced
4 garlic cloves, sliced

1 fresno chile, seeded and sliced
1 cup dry white wine
1 cup fresh orange juice
3 cups Chicken Stock (page 131)
12 black oil-cured olives, pitted and chopped
½ cup chopped fresh flat-leaf parsley leaves
2 tablespoons chestnut honey
1 cup toasted sliced almonds (see Symon Says, page 69)

Preheat the oven to 225°F.

Put a 6-quart Dutch oven over medium heat. Season the rabbit thighs with salt, pepper, and the coriander and then dredge in the flour, shaking off excess. Add the oil to the Dutch oven. Working in batches if necessary, brown the thighs for about 2 minutes per side. Remove them to a large plate. Add the onion, garlic, chile, almonds, and a pinch of salt to the Dutch oven, and sauté until the vegetables and almonds begin to brown, 4 to 5 minutes. Add the wine, orange juice, and stock, making sure to scrape the bottom of the pan with a wooden spoon. Return the thighs to the Dutch oven and bring the liquid to a simmer. Cover the pan, transfer to the oven, and braise for 3 hours, or until the meat is very tender.

Remove the thighs from the pot. Over medium heat, return the sauce to a simmer and whisk in the olives, parsley, and honey. Return the thighs to the pot to reheat and then serve.

SYMON SAYS

This dish, like most braised dishes, is best if it's made a day or two before serving so that it can cool in its cooking liquid, which enhances its flavor and its delicate texture.

BRAISED SHORT RIBS
WITH PICKLED GREEN TOMATOES

My chef de cuisine at Lola, Derek Clayton, makes these short ribs, and they are the best I've ever had. I love them topped with pickled tomatoes, a sharp contrast to the richness of the meat. They'd also be beautiful, though, with Soft Polenta with Mascarpone (page 160).

The keys to these short ribs are seasoning them a day before cooking them, cooking them on the bone, cooking them until they're tender but not mushy, and allowing them to cool in their cooking liquid, which they will reabsorb. All these steps give them a great depth of flavor. We take them off the bone and trim them before serving and we save the trim to mix with the stuffing for Beef Cheek Pierogies (see page 45).

Serves 6

6 pounds meaty beef short ribs on the bone	½ cup tomato paste
Kosher salt and freshly ground black pepper	5 sprigs of fresh thyme
	3 salt-packed anchovy fillets, rinsed
4 tablespoons olive oil	1 bay leaf
2 celery stalks, coarsely chopped	1 head of garlic, cloves peeled
1 carrot, peeled and coarsely chopped	1 quart (4 cups) Chicken Stock (page 131)
1 large onion, coarsely chopped	2 cups dry red wine
1 fresno chile, halved	⅓ cup red wine vinegar
	Pickled Green Tomatoes (page 122)

The day before cooking the short ribs, season them with salt and pepper and refrigerate.

The next day, remove the ribs from the refrigerator 30 minutes before you want to cook them.

Preheat the oven to 325°F.

Heat 2 tablespoons of the olive oil in a large enameled cast-iron Dutch oven over medium-high heat. Add half of the short ribs to the pan and cook on all sides until browned, a few minutes for each side. Transfer the ribs to a plate. Repeat with the remaining oil and ribs.

Pour off all but 2 or 3 tablespoons of fat from the pan. Add the celery, carrot, onion, and chile to the pan along with a large pinch of salt, and cook over medium heat until softened, about 7 minutes. Add the tomato paste and cook, stirring, until glossy, about 2 minutes. Add the thyme sprigs, anchovies, bay leaf, and garlic and cook, stirring, for 2 minutes. Add the stock, wine, and vinegar and bring to a boil. Return the short ribs to the pan, cover, and braise in the oven for 1 hour.

Lower the oven temperature to 225°F and cook for 4 hours, or until the meat is very tender. Remove the ribs to a large bowl and strain the liquid into the bowl. Discard the solids. Refrigerate overnight.

To serve, skim the congealed fat off the liquid and reheat the ribs in the liquid. Remove the ribs to a serving platter and cover to keep warm while you simmer the liquid to reduce it by half. Pour the sauce over the ribs and top them with the pickled tomatoes.

Fresh Bacon: The Glories of Braised Pork Belly

The first time I had fresh pork belly was at Gramercy Tavern when Tom Colicchio was the chef. I've had many dishes in my life that have changed how I feel about food. Colicchio's pork belly, with cranberry beans and pearl onions, was one of them and it reinforced what I've always believed: Pork is king.

I immediately returned to Lola and started trying all different ways to cook the versatile fresh belly. Once we had perfected it, we couldn't sell it to save our lives. Few people in Cleveland in 1998 understood what it was. But from the first time I had it, I knew that it would appeal to my customers. It has good textures and a great ratio of fat to meat; it's succulent and satisfying with a soulful richness. When I told Colicchio about the problem, he said, "So call it 'fresh bacon.'" We did—and it immediately started selling like crazy.

I don't think there are two better words in the English language than *pork belly*. My preference for the breed when it comes to pork belly is the heritage Duroc because it's such a fatty hog.

If you don't have a specialty butcher or meat market that carries fresh pork belly, most grocery stores can order it for you. These commercial bellies are acceptable, but they tend to be a little skinny and lean. For the best-quality pork belly, order it online (see Sources, page 250), or find a local farm that raises hogs and order it from them.

There are many different ways to cook pork belly: It can be slow roasted, cured and hot smoked (resulting in bacon), confited, or braised. My method of choice is to braise it in stock loaded with aromatics. It's already got so much fat on it, I don't think you need to poach it in more fat. Regardless of your preference, though, the main thing you need to know about it is that it's a tough muscle, so it requires long slow cooking to tenderize it.

Pork belly is best cooked, cooled in its cooking liquid, and then finished later, so it's great to prepare a few days before you serve it.

I like to sauté the braised pork belly to reheat it. It becomes crisp on the outside and stays tender and moist on the inside. Or you can cut it into lardons—1-inch-long batons that are ¼ inch wide and ¼ inch thick—and crisp them up almost like pork croutons and serve them on a frisée or spinach salad. It's also great with pickled relish and pickled vegetables, and with spicy greens such as watercress and arugula. Or you can use it as the center of a composed dish (see pages 216–219). It's nice on a sandwich, too. Think of it as you would bacon. And note that it's the first B in our BBLT (page 58).

BRAISED PORK BELLY

This basic braised pork belly can be used in any number of ways, including in Fresh Bacon with Watermelon and Haloumi (page 219) and in Braised Pork Belly with Soft Polenta and Seared Mushrooms (opposite). Or fry it up for a scrumptious addition to a frisée salad (see page 220).

To braise pork belly, I first remove the skin (I save it to add to any meat stock for incredible body, add it to stews, or confit it and fry it into cracklings). Then I give it a twenty-four-hour cure of salt, a little sugar, chilies, aromatics, and spices. Salt pulls out moisture and firms up the meat a little bit in addition to seasoning it. Then I braise it in a basic chicken stock with mirepoix, submerging the belly just up to the top layer of fat. Very easy to do—and delicious.

Makes 1½ pounds

2 pounds fresh pork belly, skin removed
2 tablespoons kosher salt
1 teaspoon sugar
1 tablespoon coriander seeds, toasted
    (see Symon Says, page 69)
1 tablespoon crushed red pepper flakes
Grated zest of 1 orange

1 red onion, sliced
1 carrot, sliced
4 garlic cloves
1 bay leaf
1 cup dry white wine
1 quart (4 cups) Chicken Stock (page 131)
1 cinnamon stick

Rinse the pork belly and pat it dry.

In a small bowl, mix together the salt, sugar, coriander, red pepper flakes, and orange zest. Coat the pork belly with the mixture and place in a resealable plastic bag. Refrigerate overnight or for up to 24 hours.

Preheat the oven to 275°F.

Remove the belly from the refrigerator, rinse off the seasonings, and pat dry.

In a large nonreactive pot, combine the onion, carrot, garlic, bay leaf, white wine, chicken stock, and cinnamon stick and bring to a simmer.

Put the belly in a Dutch oven and pour the liquid over it. Place the belly in the oven, cover, and braise for 7 hours, or until very tender.

Remove the pot from the oven and let the belly cool in the liquid. Cover and refrigerate in the poaching liquid until ready to use, up to 1 week. Drain (but do not discard) the liquid before using the belly.

BRAISED PORK BELLY WITH SOFT POLENTA AND SEARED MUSHROOMS

Once you have the braised pork belly cooked and chilled in your fridge, this is an easy and delicious winter dish. The mushrooms can be cooked and kept warm while you prepare the polenta or they can be cooked in advance and reheated after you've cooked the polenta. In any case, the polenta takes the longest time to cook. Another suggestion for this dish is to garnish it with Pickled Ramps (page 121) rather than the balsamic vinaigrette.

Serves 8

2 tablespoons canola oil
Braised Pork Belly (opposite), cut into
　　8 slabs
Soft Polenta with Mascarpone
　　(page 160)

Seared Wild Mushrooms (page 158)
½ cup Balsamic Vinaigrette (page 65)

Heat the oil in a medium sauté pan over medium heat. Add the pork belly and cook each side until crisp, about 2 minutes per side.

　Spoon the polenta into the center of each of eight plates. Lay the pork belly on top and top it with seared mushrooms. Drizzle a tablespoon of vinaigrette over each.

SYMON SAYS

Don't discard the poaching liquid when braising pork belly. Remove the fat from the top, strain the liquid (discard the solids), and use as a stock for hearty soups and stews.

FRESH BACON WITH WATERMELON AND HALOUMI

Haloumi is a salty Greek cheese that is firm enough to grill. I sauté it, put a piece of pork belly on top, and serve it with something acidic, some pickled green tomatoes and chilies or a spicy vinaigrette. The Greeks make a salad of seared or grilled haloumi (or feta) and watermelon which is a creative way to mix sweet and salty flavors. When I was eating one of these salads I thought, "Oh man, this would be so amazing with pork belly—because it's salty and sweet, and fatty." And that's where this recipe came from.

Serves 8 as a starter or 4 as a main course

2 tablespoons canola oil
Braised Pork Belly (page 216), cut into
    8 equal 1 by 1-inch pieces
8 ounces haloumi cheese, cut into
    24 pieces each about ¼ inch thick
1 cup Red Wine Vinaigrette with all
    optional ingredients included
    (page 65)

2 tablespoons finely sliced scallion, white
    and green parts
8 ounces red seedless watermelon, cut
    into 16 1-inch cubes

Heat the oil in a medium sauté pan over medium heat. Add the pork belly and cook to crisp the exteriors and heat the insides, about 4 minutes in all. Remove to a paper towel to drain.

Add the cheese to the pan and sauté to crisp one side, about a minute.

Combine the vinaigrette and the scallion in a mixing bowl. Add the pork belly, cheese, and watermelon to the vinaigrette and gently toss to coat.

Set a piece of cheese in the center of each plate. Arrange the watermelon and pork belly on top. Spoon a tablespoon of the vinaigrette over each serving.

FRISÉE WITH CRISPY PORK BELLY "CROUTONS"

This of course is a play on the traditional bistro dish, frisée and lardon salad. The "croutons" are cut from braised pork belly and deep-fried, which allows them to develop an amazingly crispy exterior while remaining tender and succulent within.

Serves 8

Canola oil, for deep-frying
Braised Pork Belly (page 216), cut into
   1-inch cubes
2 cups frisée

¼ cup pickled red onions (see page 117)
¼ cup Sherry Vinaigrette (page 66)
Kosher salt
8 poached eggs, optional

Pour enough oil into a large pot so that the oil comes 3 inches up the sides. Heat the oil to 375°F.

Deep-fry the pork belly "croutons" until crispy on the outside and hot and tender inside, about 4 minutes.

While the pork belly cooks, combine the frisée, onions, and vinaigrette in a mixing bowl and toss to combine. Season with salt.

When the pork belly is done, scoop it from the oil, allow to drain on paper towels, and then add to the frisée. Toss the salad and divide evenly among eight plates. If you like, top with a poached egg.

The Power of the Cookbook

I love a cookbook for how it makes me feel. Great cookbooks convey the passion of the author and change the way you think about food. They broaden your appreciation for this profession and they deepen your own love and passion for cooking. These are a handful of my favorite cookbooks, books that have been most meaningful to me as a cook, and I can't recommend them enough. In no particular order:

The French Laundry Cookbook, by Thomas Keller: I think a lot of people bought this because they were just plain curious about what Thomas Keller was doing out in Yountville, California; but for me, the great power of this book is not about the food or the recipes or the gorgeous photography. This book is important to me because it was the first cookbook that explicitly showed one man's absolute drive toward perfection. Until I read this book I believed that it was skill that made a chef great; but here I realized how driven you must be. We all work really hard, but Keller goes beyond anything I'd ever seen before.

The Zuni Cafe Cookbook, by Judy Rodgers: I love this book for Judy's absolute passion for food, her pure love of food, the way she writes about handling food, preparing food. A lot of chefs cook that same way and have written books, but why don't those books make you feel this passion? You read her recipes, the power of her descriptions, the thoughtfulness of her observations about food that can only come from a powerful love of food, and her joy comes through on every page.

The Art of Eating, by M. F. K. Fisher: I read this shortly after leaving culinary school, and it was a thrill to discover a book that is all about a passion for eating! Every chef I know becomes a chef in part because he or she loves to eat. I *love* to eat, and here is a whole book describing the glories of eating. It makes you hungry.

The Whole Beast: Nose to Tail Eating, by Fergus Henderson: This British chef took a segment of cooking that I've always dabbled in and went all out with it. I love to serve beef marrow and beef cheek and lamb's tongue, but Henderson describes the importance of using the entire animal in a way you don't see every day, and he explores the idea of not wasting a morsel, putting every cut to great use—a very important idea for all cooks.

White Heat, by Marco Pierre White: This book, beloved in the chef world maybe more than any other, was the first to capture the sheer energy that's in a kitchen. No one had ever seen this before in a book. And it shows how temperamental chefs can be. I'm not like that—really!—but after the book came out in 1992, whenever I would lose my temper, my partner, Doug Petkovic, would say, "Easy, White Heat." This book shows everybody what so many cooks love about their kitchens and their work.

CONFITED DUCK WITH PICKLED CHERRY SAUCE AND BRAISED ENDIVE

I love fat but it's got to be well balanced; this Lola signature dish has the perfect balance between sweet, tart, bitter, and rich. The key elements of this dish are made ahead, so this is easy to complete just before serving.

Serves 8

8 legs Duck Confit (page 110), at room temperature
1 cup Pickled Cherries (page 119), strained, with 1 cup of their juice reserved

2 cups Chicken Stock (page 131)
2 tablespoons unsalted butter, cut into pieces
1 bunch of watercress
Braised Endive with Citrus (page 152)

Preheat the oven to 300°F.

Heat a large ovenproof sauté pan (or two) over medium heat. Arrange the duck legs skin side down in the pan and crisp the skin for 3 to 4 minutes. Flip them and place in the oven for 5 minutes to heat through.

Meanwhile, combine the cherries, juice, and stock in a nonreactive saucepan over medium heat and simmer to reduce by half. With the liquid at a low simmer, whisk in the butter.

To serve, arrange the endive in the center of each plate and top with a duck leg. Spoon the sauce on top and garnish with watercress.

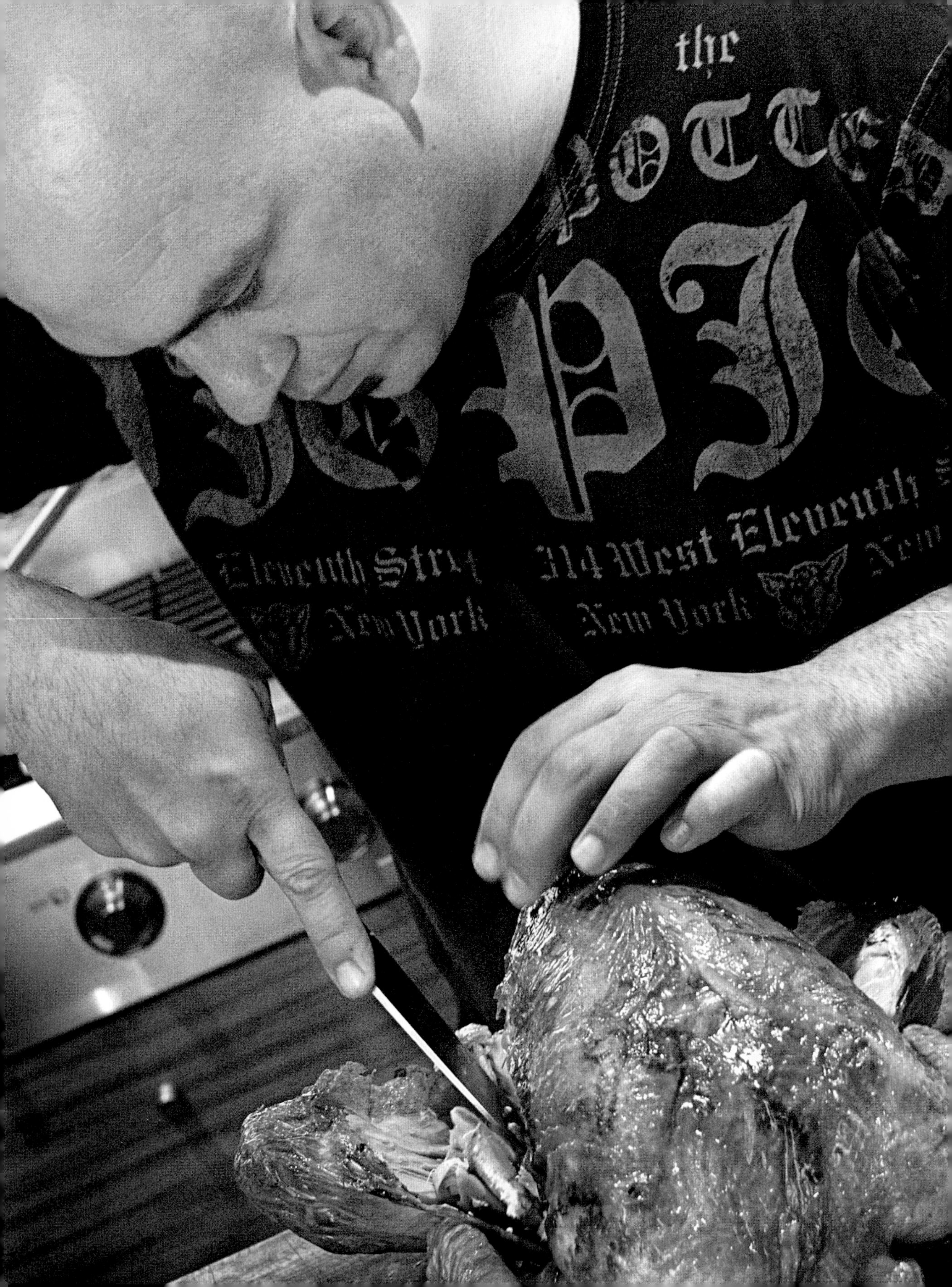
314 West Eleventh
New York

Family Meal

I could have folded these recipes into the other entrée sections but to do so would be to ignore one of the most fundamental facts of my life, the power of family, and one of my deepest convictions, that life is better when we sit down and share a meal together. We are all busy. With more dual income families and single parent families than ever, and with kids' time scheduled to the hilt, family meals may be decreasing. But I urge you, if you don't already, find at least one day a week when you and your family sit down to a meal together. I was lucky enough to do this most nights throughout my childhood and the dinner table is where I learned a lot of lessons. There's something about the dinner table that changes the way people act. We're a passionate family so there were plenty of disputes and raised voices when I was growing up, but I don't ever recall a raised voice at the dinner table, not once, unless it was a happy one. And I got punished plenty as a kid, but I was never yelled at at the dinner table. The dinner table was a special place, a safe haven, absolute comfort.

The following dishes are all big straightforward ones that remind me of childhood and family. They are meant to be served "family style," from platters and boards and pots. These are meals that are meant to be shared with a crowd, which are the best kind of meals there are.

Family

On February 11, 1998, reviewing the reservation list for that night at Lola, I noticed a 212 area code on a confirmation number. This was odd; we never had out-of-town phone numbers in our book. I'd been called by an editor of *Food & Wine* magazine several weeks earlier who'd asked me to fax a menu and we had talked a little about the food at Lola. It was good that they were paying attention to restaurants in flyover country, I thought, but that was about it. A regular customer and friend suggested we call the number or check to see if the name on the reservation appeared on the *Food & Wine* masthead. Somebody found a copy of the magazine, and yes, indeed, an associate editor shared the name on the reservation.

They were a three-top and were like any other table that night except for the fact that they ordered nearly the entire menu. I knew something was up, but not what.

And then I forgot about it. We were really busy. When *Food & Wine* called to tell me I was one of ten chosen for their Best New Chef award, I thought it was one of my buddies giving me a hard time.

The *Food & Wine* Best New Chef award resulted in a lot of changes. It altered how I was regarded on a national level. A chef from Cleveland just wasn't respected. You had to be a chef in New York, Chicago, San Francisco, or Los Angeles. Everybody being written about in the national press was in or near one of those cities. When I was at the ceremony in New York for the announcement, a chef came up to me and asked, "Who's your PR person?" I said, "I don't have one," and he said, "Impossible."

I said, "I don't have one."

"Then how the f--- would anybody find a chef in Cleveland?" The guy couldn't believe it. I don't think people in Cleveland did either. They seemed to react with the thought, "What? There's a good restaurant in Cleveland?" And people outside Cleveland definitely thought, "What? There's a good restaurant in Cleveland?!"

What it was, though, was not some sort of freak occurrence, but rather something that was happening all over the country. There were many good restaurants in Cleveland. Young chefs were returning to their hometowns and bringing good new dynamic food to an American audience that was increasingly eager for what they had to offer.

The *Food & Wine* award changed things for me personally in more ways than I probably know. Because of the national recognition, I was invited to do charity dinners in cities across the country, and the national press could write about me and not have to explain themselves. I cooked at the James Beard House in New York, and at other New York events. I caught the attention of executives at the Food Network, who had me on as a guest chef on Sara Moulton's show, and on a show called *Ready, Set, Cook*. The executives there liked me on TV and invited me to be a part of a show called *Melting Pot*. And eventually they invited me to compete on a reality cooking show that took place in three countries, and resulted in my earning a spot as an Iron Chef on *Iron Chef America*.

All this recognition feeds the restaurant and is responsible for a lot of our business. The business success leads to offers, some of which I've accepted. We closed Lola and reopened her in 2005 as a more casual Lolita, serving food in honor of my mother and her culinary heritage, turning to the freshly grilled and open-fire cooking of the Mediterranean. And I was able to build out my dream kitchen and restaurant in the center of my city, at the new Lola in 2006. I was asked to open a restaurant in New York, which received a two-star rating from Frank Bruni at the *New York Times*, who wrote that Parea was "a fittingly arresting showcase for a sophisticated chef's efforts to recast Greek cuisine by approaching it with atypically high standards, unearthing neglected traditions and finding novel assignments for commonly used ingredients." I'm proud of what we did there. Unfortunately I didn't own it, and it closed after disputes with the people who did. I've opened a restaurant in Detroit, called Roast, devoted to my favorite culinary subject: meat. And the offers continue to come.

I like the celebrity for the most part, and I don't think it's a bad thing as long as at the end of the day you know who you are. I'm still a chef and a restaurateur—that's my livelihood; that's who I am. Maybe that will change; I don't know. I think you have to be honest. Whatever recognition I have, besides driving people to my restaurants, has allowed me to continue to learn. Often what happens in the life of a chef, you get so locked into your restaurant and what you're doing that your growth almost stops. I get to travel and eat at a lot of different places and keep growing. I became a better manager because I now have to be away from my restaurants more than ever before. And this is linked to one of the most important parts of all of this for me: it's allowed me to give opportunities to my staff so that they can grow. I love that part more than anything. I love watching my staff grow.

It's that piece of the puzzle that I'd first recognized when I returned from culinary school and got a job with Mark Shary at Players: Good restaurants are families. I'm really lucky to have a great family in Lola and a business that grows so that Derek can take the reins at Lola, and Matthew can run Lolita, and Frankie Ritz can manage the Detroit restaurant, and Cory Barrett, Lola pastry chef, can open his own pâtisserie.

I grew up in a great family that loves cooking and food and Liz and I continue to live among that family: Mom's still in the restaurant working several days a week and Dad does the books, and Pap recently celebrated his ninetieth birthday at Lolita. And I continue to live within the restaurant with a family that continues to grow. I love you all.

YIA YIA'S SUNDAY SAUCE

Yia Yia, my maternal grandmother, made this exact sauce and it's the base for several dishes in this book, including Italian Braised Beef with Root Vegetables (page 232) and Pappardelle with Pig's-Head Ragù (page 88). But of course it's fantastic just served on pasta and topped with torn fresh basil.

Yia Yia was a magical woman. Born in southern Italy, she married my Papou, a Greek man, and in the Greek community where he lived he was ostracized for marrying an Italian. So Yia Yia decided to learn how to speak, read, and cook Greek. When she was ready, Papou invited all his Greek friends to a feast she'd prepared. She made Greek food better than the Greeks and because of this, they welcomed both of them back into the community. It's something that has been reinforced over and over for me: food's power to bring people together.

This red sauce reflects her Neapolitan heritage, and it uses plum tomatoes grown in San Marzano, a town outside Naples. San Marzanos are the best available; their natural sweetness makes them especially good for tomato sauces, and they are the only tomatoes used in true Neapolitan pizzas. As for all tomato-based dishes, use a stainless steel or nonreactive pan.

What makes this sauce so good is the long, slow cooking time, which allows it to develop a complex flavor. It shouldn't simmer; there should just be a bubble rising to the surface every now and then. Meaty beef bones add more depth and complexity. (If you have beef stock, you can add two cups of it in place of the bones.) My cousins and I used to get in trouble for dipping bread in the sauce while it was cooking—all day long, how can you resist?—until Yia Yia started making double batches to accommodate everyone tasting it throughout the day. I have such great memories of eating it this way, that I encourage it at my house.

This sauce is chunky with abundant tomato and sliced garlic. Depending on what you're using this for, it can be served as is (over a very thick hearty pasta or as part of a braising liquid). But if you were to use it for an angel hair or as a sauce for sautéed veal, you would probably want to purée it in a blender until it's uniformly smooth. This sauce freezes well, so you can make big batches, portion it into smaller containers, and freeze it for when you need it.

Makes 2 quarts

¼ cup olive oil
1 large Spanish onion, finely diced
6 garlic cloves, sliced
1 tablespoon kosher salt, or more to taste
2 28-ounce cans San Marzano tomatoes, with their juice
1 cup dry white wine

2 pounds meaty beef bones
1 bay leaf
1 tablespoon fresh oregano leaves
¼ teaspoon freshly ground black pepper
1 tablespoon crushed red pepper flakes (optional)

recipe continued on next page

Heat the oil in a 4-quart saucepan or large Dutch oven over medium heat. Add the onion and cook until translucent, 2 minutes. Add the garlic and salt and cook until everything is soft but not browned, about 3 minutes.

Squeeze the tomatoes one by one into the pan, pulverizing them by hand, and pour in their juice, too. Add the wine, beef bones, bay leaf, oregano, black pepper, and red pepper flakes, if using. Bring the sauce to a simmer, then reduce the heat to its lowest possible setting, and continue to cook for 8 hours. The sauce should reduce by about one third.

Taste for seasoning and add more salt if necessary. Remove the bones and bay leaf. If not using right away, let the sauce cool, then cover, and refrigerate for up to 1 week or freeze for up to 2 months.

ROASTED LEG OF LAMB WITH TZATZIKI SAUCE

This is a Greek-style classic at my house around the holidays. It used to be something we typically enjoyed around Easter time, but every now and then I'll make it at Christmas or just for a family get-together that calls for a big and festive meal. I love John and Sukey Jamison's lamb from their Jamison Farm in Pennsylvania (see Sources, page 250).

Serves 8

6 shallots, minced (about ¾ cup)
4 garlic cloves, minced
¼ cup chopped fresh rosemary
2 tablespoons sugar
2 tablespoons coriander seeds, toasted
  and crushed (see Symon Says,
  page 69)

1 tablespoon crushed red pepper flakes
1½ tablespoons kosher salt
1 6-pound bone-in leg of lamb
Tzatziki Sauce (page 141)

Mix together in a medium bowl the shallots, garlic, rosemary, sugar, coriander, red pepper flakes, and salt. Rub the mixture all over the surface of the lamb. Place in a large glass baking dish, cover with plastic wrap, and refrigerate overnight.

Remove the lamb from the baking dish, rinse off the seasonings, and pat dry. Let the lamb sit at room temperature for 1 hour.

Preheat the oven to 375°F.

Heat a roasting pan or large ovenproof skillet over medium heat. Add the lamb and brown on all sides, 7 to 10 minutes. Transfer the lamb, fat side up, to a roasting rack set into a roasting pan. Roast until the lamb reaches an internal temperature of 140°F, about 1½ hours.

Remove the lamb from the pan and set it aside to rest for 20 minutes.

Slice the lamb and serve with the tzatziki sauce.

ITALIAN BRAISED BEEF WITH ROOT VEGETABLES

My mom, Angel, has always been the best cook in the neighborhood and everybody knew it. In the 1970s and '80s, when most of my friends were eating fast food and processed junk, all the kids wanted to come to my house for dinner. (We weren't going to go to the neighbors' houses to eat TV dinners.) This is one of the meals Mom would fix when I was growing up because it was easy, delicious and inexpensive, and it fed a crowd.

This was my introduction to braising, the first braised dish I ever made—and I didn't even know we were braising. Mom called it pot roast and we had it weekly. And in true Italian pot roast fashion, we'd eat it over rigatoni. I now sometimes serve it over Soft Polenta with Mascarpone (page 160), another excellent option. It showed me how much I loved the deep complex flavors of braises generally, which I prefer to eat over just about any other kind of dish. One of the pleasures of this meal is the big chunks of carrots and celery root that cook in that delicious liquid for four hours; they take on all the flavors of the braising liquid. They don't taste like carrots and celery root anymore; they taste like a steak, and that's why they're so good.

A couple of critical steps in this recipe are getting a good sear on the meat and caramelizing the vegetables in the pot before deglazing. Beyond that, the red sauce is critical. And I also think it's important that a third of the meat be above the liquid—one of the factors that for me defines braising—so pot size is important; it shouldn't be so small that the meat is submerged or so big that the meat is sitting in just an inch of liquid.

Serves 6

3 pounds rump roast
Kosher salt and freshly ground black
    pepper
3 tablespoons olive oil
1 carrot, peeled and cut into 1-inch
    chunks
1 onion, coarsely chopped

1 small celery root, peeled and cut into
    1-inch chunks
4 garlic cloves, minced
1 cup red wine
2 cups Yia Yia's Sunday Sauce (page 229)
2 bay leaves

Preheat the oven to 300°F.

Season the meat liberally with salt and pepper, as much as a day in advance. (Cover and refrigerate it if doing so and take the meat out of the fridge 30 minutes before cooking.) Heat the oil in a large Dutch oven over high heat. When the oil is on the verge of smoking, sear the meat, about 2 minutes on each side. Move the meat to the side (or remove it from the pot altogether if necessary), and add the carrot, onion, and celery root. Brown the vegetables, about 3 minutes, then add the garlic and cook for a minute or two longer.

Add the wine to deglaze the pot, scraping up the browned bits on the bottom. Add the tomato sauce, 1 cup water, and the bay leaves (and the pot roast if you removed it). Bring the liquid to a simmer and taste for seasoning. Add more salt if necessary. Cover the pot and place it in the oven for 3 hours, basting the meat occasionally during this time.

Discard the bay leaves before serving. The meat can be removed to a cutting board and sliced if you're serving individual plates, or the meat can be pulled apart with a couple of forks right in the pot at the table and served with plenty of the sauce and vegetables.

MOM'S LASAGNA

Every Wednesday at my parents' house was lasagna night. This was the night all my friends begged to eat over; the dish cemented my mom, Angel, as best cook on the street. (That's Angel on the facing page, working the reservation book at Lolita.) You could smell the lasagna baking houses away, and Wednesday was the only night of the week that I was more than happy to come in from outside and be early for dinner. I've eaten lasagna in every corner of the earth and I have yet to find one as good as Mom's.

Serves 8

½ cup olive oil
1 onion, diced
4 garlic cloves, minced
Kosher salt
1 pound pork neck bones
1 pound ground veal
1 pound ground beef
1 pound spicy Italian sausage, loose or
    removed from the casing
½ cup dry white wine
4 cups chopped peeled tomatoes, or
    1 28-ounce can San Marzano
    tomatoes, with their juice

3 bay leaves
1 pound dried lasagna noodles
2 pounds whole-milk ricotta cheese
¼ cup chopped fresh flat-leaf parsley
    leaves
¼ cup chopped fresh basil leaves
¼ cup chopped fresh oregano leaves
2 large eggs
1 pound fresh mozzarella cheese, grated
½ cup grated Parmesan cheese

In a large Dutch oven or heavy pot, heat the olive oil over medium heat. Add the onion, garlic, and a three-finger pinch of salt and sweat them until they're translucent, 2 minutes. Add the neck bones and brown them, about 5 minutes. Add the ground veal and beef and sausage, season with another healthy pinch of salt, and continue cooking until the meat is browned, about 10 minutes. Add the white wine, tomatoes and their juice, and the bay leaves, scraping the bottom of the pot with a wooden spoon, making sure to get all of the browned bits into the sauce. Season the sauce with salt and simmer for 2 hours over medium heat. Remove the bay leaves and neck bones and let cool. Skim any fat that rises to the surface.

Bring a large pot of water to a boil. Add enough salt so that it tastes seasoned and allow the water to return to a boil. Add the noodles and cook until al dente. Drain well and set aside.

Meanwhile, in a medium bowl mix together the ricotta, parsley, basil, oregano, and eggs with a pinch of salt.

Preheat the oven to 350°F.

In a lasagna pan—9 by 13 inches is optimal—ladle about 1 cup sauce on the bottom. Arrange a layer of noodles on this followed by a layer of sauce and then some of the ricotta mixture, smoothing it with a spatula to the edges. Repeat the process until the pan is full. Finish with a final layer of noodles, sauce, the mozzarella, and Parmesan.

Cover the lasagna with aluminum foil and bake for 1 hour. Uncover and bake for 30 minutes. Let cool for 30 minutes before cutting and serving.

"CLEVELAND-STYLE" CLAMBAKE

A little known fact: Cleveland is the clambake capital of the country. I don't know why this is, but my fish purveyors tell me that from August through September they sell more clams to Cleveland than to any other city in the country.

My interpretation of the clambake is not traditional; it's done more in the style of a crab boil, with sausage, corn, clams, and shrimp all layered in a pot and cooked together. To serve this, I dump the whole pot out onto a table lined with newspaper or a plastic tablecloth. You can put it in a big serving bowl, but the effect of dumping it out onto a table is stunning. I learned the service trick from Susie Heller, former Clevelander and a coauthor on numerous wonderful books, and I prepared this clambake on *Dinner Impossible;* we made six huge vats to serve four hundred people. But it's a no-brainer, and it's one of the best, most dramatic one-pot family meals there is.

Serves 8

1 pound smoked kielbasa, sliced in ½-inch disks
2 ears of corn, cut into 8 pieces
3½ pounds littleneck clams
1 pound shell-on medium (16- to 20-count) shrimp
2 tablespoons coriander seeds, toasted (page 69)
1 tablespoon cumin seeds, toasted (page 69)
1 tablespoon kosher salt
1 medium onion, thinly sliced
1 head of garlic, cloves peeled and thinly sliced
2 fresno chilies, thinly sliced into rings
1 tablespoon crushed red pepper flakes
1 bay leaf
1 lemon, cut in thirds
1 750-ml bottle dry white wine
1 cup fresh cilantro leaves

In a large pot with a lid, add the food in layers—the sausage first, followed by the corn, clams, and shrimp. Distribute the coriander, cumin, salt, onion, garlic, chilies, red pepper flakes, bay leaf, and lemon over the top. Pour in the wine, cover, and cook over high heat until the clams open, 20 to 25 minutes. Discard the bay leaf and any clams that do not open. Sprinkle with cilantro before serving.

LIZZIE'S ROASTED CHICKEN WITH SALSA VERDE

You didn't hear it from me, but when Liz and I started dating she wasn't the greatest of cooks. She almost took me out twice—once with some not-so-fresh crayfish and the other time with some medium-rare chicken. Now she is a whiz in the kitchen and makes a mean roasted chicken. People will always say: Of course she can cook; she's married to a chef! (But as any husband knows, she would have to listen to me to learn from me!) Liz learned all on her own mainly because she is not afraid to make mistakes and will try anything. This is a great lesson for anyone who is learning to cook. You will definitely make mistakes along the way, but if you keep at it eventually you'll figure it out. Just make sure not to take anyone out on the way!

Serves 4

1 3- to 4-pound chicken
1 tablespoon kosher salt
1 lemon, thinly sliced and seeded
2 fresh bay leaves
1 small onion, peeled

3 garlic cloves
1 small bunch of fresh thyme
2 tablespoons olive oil
Salsa Verde (opposite)

A day before cooking, rinse the chicken inside and out under cold water and pat dry. Salt it liberally, cover, and refrigerate.

Remove the chicken from the refrigerator an hour before cooking it.

Preheat the oven to 425°F.

Lift the skin off each chicken breast and wedge 3 lemon slices and a bay leaf between the skin and each breast. Put the onion, garlic, thyme, and remaining lemon in the cavity of the chicken. Rub the entire chicken liberally with the olive oil. Put the chicken in an ovenproof sauté pan or in a roasting pan breast side up, slide it into the oven, and roast it until the thigh reaches 160°F or until the cavity juices run clear, about 1 hour.

Remove from the oven and let rest for 10 to 20 minutes. Cut the chicken into 8 pieces and serve with the salsa verde.

SALSA VERDE

Makes 1¼ cups

¼ cup thinly sliced fresh flat-leaf parsley
2 tablespoons thinly sliced fresh mint
2 salt-packed anchovy fillets, rinsed and
    minced
1 garlic clove, minced
1 shallot, minced
Grated zest and juice of 1 lemon
2 tablespoons salt-packed capers, rinsed
    and chopped

1 jalapeño, seeded and minced (about
    1 tablespoon)
½ teaspoon crushed red pepper flakes
½ cup extra-virgin olive oil
Kosher salt and freshly ground black
    pepper

Combine the parsley, mint, anchovies, garlic, shallot, lemon zest and juice, capers, jalapeño, red pepper flakes, and olive oil in a bowl and stir to combine. Add salt and pepper to taste.

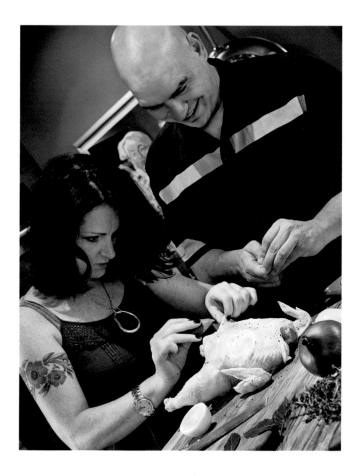

TURKEY 101

Classes on how to roast a turkey sell out faster than any of the other classes I give at my restaurant, Lolita. In the fall, it's the main question I get from people: How do I roast a turkey? So here's how I do it and always end up with a beautiful, golden-brown bird that's completely cooked and juicy inside.

One of the main mistakes people make is buying a bird that's too big. I recommend you buy a ten- to twelve-pound bird, and if that's not enough buy two birds rather than one bigger one. Turkey is the one animal of which I don't prefer to use heritage breeds; I find them to be tough and dry.

To cook the bird, you'll need a large roasting pan and cheesecloth to cover the entire breast. Season the bird a day in advance with plenty of salt, about two tablespoons for a ten-pound bird. I never fill the carcass with a stuffing; when you do, you have to overcook the bird in order to fully cook the stuffing. If you want to serve a stuffing, bake it separately. Instead fill the cavity with aromatic vegetables and herbs, such as onion and fennel, which perfume the meat and keep the bird moist.

I melt butter with herbs and soak a piece of cheesecloth in the butter. I then drape this over the turkey to keep it moist and ensure that the turkey will be a perfect golden brown every time. I roast it in a hot oven until the juices run clear and, finally, let it rest for at least fifteen to twenty minutes to finish cooking and allow the juices to redistribute themselves.

And that's all there is to it. There's no reason to think that cooking a turkey is tricky or difficult.

Serves 6 to 7

One 10-pound turkey (neck and gizzards reserved)
2 tablespoons kosher salt
1 head of garlic, halved through its equator
4 sprigs of fresh oregano
4 sprigs of fresh thyme

1 lemon, quartered
1 onion, peeled and quartered
1 fennel bulb, quartered
¼ cup picked fennel fronds
8 tablespoons (1 stick) unsalted butter
¼ cup Chicken Stock (page 131) or turkey stock or water

The day before roasting, rinse the turkey inside and out with cold water, set on a clean kitchen towel, and pat dry. Season the turkey inside and out with the salt. Wrap the turkey in plastic wrap and refrigerate for 24 hours.

Remove the turkey from the refrigerator 1 to 2 hours prior to roasting to bring to room temperature.

Preheat the oven to 425°F with the oven rack set on the lowest rung.

In the turkey's neck cavity, place a few cloves of the garlic, a few sprigs of oregano, a few sprigs of thyme, and a quarter of the lemon. Wrap the neck skin over and around the cavity to enclose the seasoning ingredients. In the body cavity, place half of the remaining garlic, half of the onion, half of the fennel, the fennel fronds, 2 lemon quarters, and half of the remaining oregano and thyme. Place the turkey, breast side up, on a rack set into a large roasting pan. Fold the wings and tuck the tips underneath the bird.

In a saucepan over medium heat, melt the butter. Add the remaining garlic, onion, fennel, lemon, oregano, and thyme to the pot with the stock or water. Bring to a boil, reduce the heat so that the liquid simmers, and continue to cook at a low simmer for 10 minutes. Remove from the heat and allow to cool slightly. When cool enough to handle, soak a double layer of cheesecloth big enough to cover the bird in the butter mixture and drape over the breast and legs of the turkey. Pour the remaining contents of the pan over the bird, pushing the pieces of vegetable and herbs into the bottom of the roasting pan. Add the neck and gizzards to the bottom of the roasting pan.

Place the turkey in the oven and roast for 45 minutes (there will be the distinct possibility of smoke depending on how clean your oven is). Turn the oven temperature down to 375°F, and continue to roast for another 15 to 20 minutes (removing the cheesecloth for the final 10 minutes to brown, if needed), or until an instant-read thermometer inserted into the center of a thigh registers 160°F. Remove the turkey from the oven and allow to rest for 20 minutes before carving.

ROASTED RACK OF PORK WITH GRILLED PEACHES AND CHESTNUT HONEY VINAIGRETTE

Pork and peaches are a great combination—and these peaches pick up extra flavor from being grilled. This vinaigrette uses my favorite kind of honey, chestnut honey (see Sources, page 250). Bees that populate chestnut orchards produce a honey that has a slight bitterness and distinct savory notes. It's a perfect pair with pork, but wildflower honey will work as well.

Serves 8

1 6-pound center-cut rack of pork, not Frenched
Kosher salt
1 tablespoon minced garlic
3 tablespoons minced shallot
2 tablespoons chestnut honey
⅓ cup balsamic vinegar

½ cup plus 2 tablespoons extra-virgin olive oil
1 tablespoon coriander seeds, toasted and crushed (see Symon Says, page 69)
¼ cup sliced fresh cilantro leaves
Grated zest and juice of 1 orange
4 to 6 peaches, halved and pitted

A day before cooking, season the pork liberally with salt, cover, and refrigerate.

Remove the pork from the refrigerator at least 30 minutes before cooking it.

Build a hot fire in an outdoor grill.

To make the vinaigrette, in a small bowl, combine the garlic and shallot and toss them with 1 teaspoon salt. Add the honey and vinegar, then whisk in ½ cup of the olive oil. Add the coriander, cilantro, and orange zest and juice.

When the coals are ready, spread them over half of the grill so that one side of the grill will be cooler than the other. Place the grill grate over the coals and allow it to get hot.

Brush the pork with the remaining 2 tablespoons olive oil. Grill the pork directly over the hot coals, turning it to sear on all sides, about 15 minutes. Move the pork to the cooler side of the grill, cover the grill, and cook the pork until it reaches an internal temperature of 145°F, about 40 minutes. Remove the pork to a cutting board. Let it rest for 5 to 10 minutes.

While the pork is resting, toss the peach halves in the vinaigrette. Grill them over high heat until charred and tender, about 2 minutes per side. Return them to the vinaigrette once they have been grilled.

Slice the pork into chops, arrange the pieces on a board or platter, and spoon the peaches and vinaigrette over the pork.

SYMON SAYS

My basic balsamic is a twenty-year-old La Piana I buy at Whole Foods, but there are many available at varying prices; I recommend you look for one with an acidity level of 6 to 7 percent.

PORK CHEEK CHILI

I love pork and I try to use it whenever I can. For this chili I use pork cheeks, the well-marbled muscle from the jowl. It braises very rich and tender with a great texture and makes a fabulous chili.

Serves 12 to 14

4 teaspoons coriander seeds, toasted and ground (see Symon Says, page 69; 1 tablespoon)

1 tablespoon sweet smoked paprika

1 teaspoon ground cumin

5 pounds pork cheeks or pork shoulder, cleaned, trimmed, and cubed

Kosher salt and freshly ground black pepper

4 tablespoons extra-virgin olive oil

1 pound slab bacon, cut into ½-inch dice

1 onion, finely chopped

3 garlic cloves, minced

2 jalapeño chilies, seeded and very finely chopped

2 red bell peppers, cored, seeded, and finely diced

1 12-ounce bottle amber ale or porter

2 cups Chicken Stock (page 131)

1 28-ounce can San Marzano tomatoes, with their juice

2 canned chipotles in adobo, seeded and minced

1 pound dried black-eyed peas (1⅔ cups), picked over and rinsed

1 small cinnamon stick

Shredded smoked cheddar cheese, for garnish

Fresh cilantro leaves, for garnish

Sliced scallions, white and green parts, for garnish

Crème fraîche, for garnish

In a large bowl, combine the coriander, paprika, and cumin and toss with the pork cheeks. Season with salt and pepper.

In a large enameled cast-iron Dutch oven, heat 2 tablespoons of the oil over medium-high heat. Add half of the pork and cook, turning as needed, until browned on all sides, about 8 minutes. Transfer the pork to a plate. Add the remaining 2 tablespoons of oil and brown the remaining pork. Transfer to the plate. Add the bacon to the pot and cook over medium heat, stirring occasionally, until browned and slightly crisp, about 7 minutes. Add the onion, garlic, jalapeños, and bell peppers and cook, stirring occasionally, until the vegetables are softened, about 5 minutes.

Return the pork cheeks to the pot along with any accumulated juices. Add the ale, chicken stock, tomatoes, chipotles, black-eyed peas, and cinnamon stick and bring to a boil. Cover and cook over very low heat until the meat and beans are tender, about 2½ hours.

Season the chili with salt and pepper. Spoon off the fat from the surface and discard the cinnamon stick. Serve the chili in bowls. Pass the smoked cheddar, cilantro, scallions, and crème fraîche at the table.

SPLIT PEA SOUP WITH BACON, HAM HOCK, AND SPARE RIBS

This is the dish that started my lifelong affinity for all things pork. Most weekends of my childhood, Pap, my dad's dad, would take me to Cleveland's West Side Market, a spectacular indoor market built in 1912 that still is what it was then, home to scores of vendors selling all manner of meats—sausages, pâtés, hams, even pig's heads and lamb hearts—as well as fish, vegetables, spices, nuts, and dairy. At the market, he'd buy ham hocks, a side of ribs, a slab of bacon, and whatever else we'd need, then stop by Higbee's department store, connected to the Terminal Tower in downtown Cleveland, to pick up my grandma. The wonderful smell of smoked pig parts filled his big old Lincoln on our way to their house on the city's east side.

This is a fall/winter dish, so I associate it with football, which we'd watch as we cooked all day. First Pap would brown the ribs in the bacon fat, and he'd throw in the chopped vegetables, then the ham hock and the split peas, cover everything with water, and simmer it for hours. From the moment that first bacon began to render, the whole house smelled all weekend of great food being cooked.

You don't need to have homemade stock for this, and you wouldn't want to adulterate it with store-bought broth. Water is all you need; the soup picks up the sweetness of the vegetables and the smoky rich flavors of the pork and it gets body from the connective tissue in the hock and ribs. It's a great hearty soup. Pap would remove the hock, pick off the meat, and add the meat back to the soup. He didn't purée it; he left the tender split peas intact. He'd pour it all into a big bowl, and at the table we'd scoop out ribs into our bowls and ladle in the chunky soup, which we'd devour with a big hunk of crusty bread. I get hungry thinking about it. There's no better food in the world.

Serves 8 to 10

4 ounces slab bacon, finely diced (½ cup)
1 slab of pork spare ribs, cut into
    individual pieces (16 to 20 ribs)
1 small carrot, peeled and finely diced
1 red onion, finely diced
1 celery stalk, finely diced
1 tablespoon kosher salt, or more to taste
1 pound split peas (1⅓ cups)

1 garlic clove, minced
1 bay leaf
1 tablespoon fresh thyme leaves
1 smoked ham hock
1 teaspoon cayenne pepper
1 teaspoon freshly cracked black pepper
Crusty bread, for serving

Sauté the bacon in a 6-quart Dutch oven over medium-low heat until the fat has rendered and it's cooked, 5 to 10 minutes. Remove the bacon to a plate with a slotted spoon, increase the heat under the pot to medium, and add the ribs. Brown on both sides, 3 minutes per side. Remove the ribs to a plate and set aside.

Add the carrot, onion, celery, and salt and sweat the vegetables for about 3 minutes. Add the split peas, garlic, bay leaf, thyme, ham hock, cayenne pepper, black pepper, the ribs, and 2½ quarts water. Simmer, skimming the foam that will rise to the surface as the water comes up to heat, until the peas and spare ribs are tender, 2 to 3 hours.

Discard the bay leaf. Remove the hock from the soup. When it's cool enough to handle, pick the meat off it and add it back to the soup (discard the bone).

To serve, divide the ribs among bowls and ladle the soup over them. Eat with abundant crusty bread.

SOURCES

For bacon
Nueske's
Rural Route #2, P.O. Box D
Wittenberg, WI 54499
800-392-2226
www.nueskes.com

For fresh pork belly and pork fatback
Niman Ranch
1600 Harbor Bay Parkway
Suite 250
Alameda, CA 94502
510-808-0330
www.nimanranch.com

For all sausage and curing supplies, including casings, sausage stuffer, and pink salt, sold here under the brand name DQ Curing Salt
Butcher & Packer
1468 Gratiot Avenue
Detroit, MI 48207
313-567-1250 or 800-521-3188
www.butcher-packer.com

For duck fat, foie gras, and other fowl pleasures
D'Artagnan
280 Wilson Avenue
Newark, NJ 07105
800-327-8246
www.dartagnan.com

For lamb
Jamison Farm
171 Jamison Lane
Latrobe, PA 15650
800-237-5262
www.jamisonfarm.com

For polenta and other organic heirloom grains
Anson Mills
1922-C Gervais Street
Columbia, SC 29201
803-467-4122
www.ansonmills.com

For barrel-aged feta
Mt. Vikos, Inc.
1291 Ocean Street
Marshfield, MA 02050
781-834-0828
Mt. Vikos products are available online:
www.salumeriaitaliana.com

For sheep's milk ricotta
Pastacheese
153 7th Street
Garden City, NY 11530
800-386-9198
www.pastacheese.com

For Roth Käse Buttermilk Blue cheese
Roth Käse
657 Second Street
P.O. Box 319
Monroe, WI 53566
608-329-7666
www.rothkase.com

For chestnut honey
Eurogrocer
304 Main Avenue, #363
Norwalk, CT 06851
888-490-8781
www.eurogrocer.com

INDEX

Note: Page references in *italics* refer to photographs.